Pictorial History
of
American Presidents

Pictorial History
of
American Presidents

by

John and Alice Durant

A. S. Barnes and Company   New York

Published on the same day in the Dominion of Canada by THE COPP CLARK COMPANY, LTD., TORONTO

Contents

CONTENTS

Introduction

Americans have found their presidents and life in the White House sources of never-ending interest. In part this derives from the people's fascination with the man they themselves have raised to such power and with the symbol of the times they have created. There is a touch of the old magic which surrounded kings in our concept of the Presidency; we sense it most, perhaps, at the change of administrations when the man who rides to the Capitol as President of the United States returns from it as a plain citizen, the magic having passed to his successor.

Behind the power and mystery of great office is, however, a man, a man who loves and hates, stumbles and strides, a man who shapes or is shaped by his times and countrymen. Great events find this man at the center of the vortex, but also in strange and unexpected ways his name becomes associated with all sorts of events on the far fringes of importance.

John and Alice Durant, who have already given us the *Pictorial History of American Ships* and, with Otto Bettmann, the *Pictorial History of American Sports,* have kept in mind these varied and sometimes contradictory aspects of the Presidency as they created this volume. For two years they worked their way through the books, manuscripts, periodicals and picture collections of a score of libraries and museums, to produce a book which would help us to see our presidents as men, as statesmen, and as the dominant symbols of their periods. The plan which they have followed generally throughout the book is something like this: first, a biographical sketch that gives a sense of the character, appearance and personality of each president and a glimpse of his wife. Then come the great events—the wars and political struggles, the monumental movements of our people forward during the administration of that particular leader. Then the lesser events, the fads, fires, scandals, crimes, the men and women whose names were on every tongue.

Pictorial histories are a new thing in the land, and they present their authors with some special problems and their readers (or lookers) with some interesting questions of evaluation. For example, to be successful there must be a merging and interdependence of text and pictures so that the impact is unified—and this unity, I believe, the Durants have achieved. As in any book, of course, the authors must decide for whom the book is designed. The Durants have deliberately chosen to produce a popular book, and while such paraphernalia dear to the scholars as a comprehensive index and a complete notation of the source of every one of the 566 pictures are included, yet they have permitted themselves freedoms of choice which would not be possible if they foresaw scholars rather than the general public as their readers. On a few occasions they have used pictures which are not contemporary with the event—Grant Wood's painting of Washington cutting down the cherry tree, for example. Critics can quarrel with this if they want to, but the Durants have made their choices with their eyes wide open in the belief that the end result will be a more lively and entertaining book. And this choice, it seems to me, is in keeping with the chatty, informal style with which they have presented their facts. On the other hand, their casual style should not lead anyone to assume that there is any casualness about the

research that is the sound backbone of the book, research which has been done with exacting care and thoroughness.

Another interesting problem facing the authors of pictorial histories is the choice of pictures: to choose the telling, significant picture which can say better than words what needs to be said. Happily, these authors have used paintings, prints, cartoons, photographs, most of them not generally known and a few of them (*e.g.* the caricature of Washington on page 21, Winslow Homer's unfinished sketch of Lincoln, Tad and Grant on page 149) almost unknown even to the specialists.

One final word of caution. Read the pictures as carefully as you do the text, exploring the details, considering the artistic medium and keeping in mind the special problems of that medium. Let your mind explore with your eyes, searching the pictures until you really see them, for too few of us have learned how to see what our eyes look at. And the pictures in this volume will repay your searching—for not only do they tell of our presidents, they tell of ourselves.

Louis C. Jones, Director
New York State Historical Association

Pictorial History
of
American Presidents

GEORGE WASHINGTON 1732–1799

President 1789–1797

George Washington was a giant among men in more ways than one. Physically he was huge for his day, standing six feet, two inches. He was broad-shouldered, muscular, and had enormous hands and feet (size thirteen). In the prime of life he weighed two hundred pounds. Fair of complexion, he had brown hair, penetrating blue eyes, a large straight nose and a firm yet pleasant mouth. Always he possessed an indefinable grace and dignity which impressed all men who knew him.

Most people visualize him as looking like the Gilbert Stuart portrait (the one on the dollar bill) because it is the most reproduced. Other artists saw him differently. One who did was the Swedish court painter, Adolf Ulric Wertmüller, whose conception of Washington as he looked at the age of sixty-two appears on the opposite page. Rarely reproduced, it brings out in detail the ruffled lace, the powder from the well-groomed wig sprinkling the velvet coat, and shows an unusually narrow forehead.

It was painted at Washington's request and is an exact replica of the one Wertmüller did from life the year before.

The first three years of George Washington's life were spent in his birthplace (above) on Pope's Creek, Wakefield, Virginia. Contrary to popular opinion George was not born with a silver spoon in his mouth. His father, Augustine, was a land-poor planter. When he died in 1743 he left his wife and children five thousand acres of land, twenty-two slaves and not much else.

George's birth record is shown below as it appeared in an old family Bible in his father's handwriting. The inscription states that the boy was born "ye 11th day of February." Twenty years after the record was made the British government ordered the Gregorian calendar, or "new style" as it was called, to be adopted. The deficiency was then eleven days and these were added. Thus, February 22 is now celebrated as Washington's birthday.

George Washington, son to Augustine & Mary his wife was born ye 11 Day of February 173½ about 10 in the Morning & was baptis'd the 3ᵈ of April following Mr. Beverley Whiting & Capt. Christopher Brooks godfathers and Mrs. Mildred Gregory godmother;

3

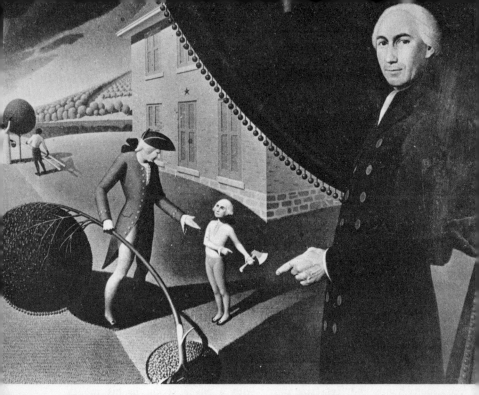

"Parson" Weems was the man responsible for the hatchet and cherry tree myth. An itinerant bookseller and preacher, the Parson (Mason Locke Weems) published in 1800 the first biography of Washington. It met with such success that he enlarged it in later editions and included some stories supposedly gleaned from relatives and neighbors who had known the great man in childhood. The cherry tree yarn did not appear until the fifth edition, published in 1806. Parson Weems explained vaguely that the story was told to him twenty years before by an aged lady who was a distant relative of the Washingtons. At any rate, this is how the Parson wrote it:

" 'I can't tell a lie, pa; you know I can't tell a lie. I did it with my hatchet.'

" 'Run to my arms, you dearest boy,' cried his father in transport; 'run to my arms; glad am I, George, that you killed my tree, for you have paid me a thousandfold. Such an act of heroism in my son is worth more than a thousand trees, though blossomed with silver, and their fruits of purest gold.' "

This fanciful painting above by Grant Wood shows little George with the Gilbert Stuart head, father Augustine in transport, and Parson Weems drawing back the curtain to reveal the episode.

After his father's death young George grew up mostly in the homes of his half brothers, being a poor relation and dependent upon their bounty. His favorite home was Mount Vernon, which his oldest brother, Lawrence, had inherited. There he learned the rudiments of surveying and at sixteen made his first trip into the wilderness to survey a vast tract of land in the valley of Virginia. For the next three years he led the rugged life of a frontiersman. He was a good surveyor and kept accurate account of his findings, an example of which is shown here. (Not long ago the United States government retraced his lines and found them remarkably correct.)

George was only twenty-one when Robert Dinwiddie, the colony's royal Governor, sent him west to warn the French at Fort Le Boeuf (near Waterford, Pennsylvania) not to encroach on British crown land. On the way back, George almost lost his life while crossing the frigid waters of the Allegheny River on a raft built by himself and his guide, Christopher Gist (below). George was jerked overboard, but managed to swim to

a small island where the two men spent the night in the freezing midwinter cold. Next day they walked across the river on solid ice. The French said no to Dinwiddie's demands.

George had another narrow escape from death two years later when he served as aide to General Edward Braddock in an expedition against the French at Fort Duquesne (Pittsburgh). Braddock was a sixty-year-old veteran of the Anglo-German military school, who knew nothing about Indian warfare. The result, when his force was ambushed in the Monongahela forests, was a complete rout (above). Washington, weak from a "violent illness," had ridden twelve hours before reaching the scene of battle. Two horses were shot from under him and four bullets tore through his clothes. Braddock received mortal wounds in the shoulder and chest. Four days later they buried him in the middle of the road as Washington conducted the service. Then the retreating wagons passed over the grave, obliterating all signs of it so that the Indians could not find the body for its prized scalp.

Short and slight, with brown eyes, Martha Dandridge Custis was a rich widow with two children when she married George on January 6, 1759.

This is the first portrait of Washington. Painted by C. W. Peale in 1772 when George was forty, it shows him as a colonel wearing the uniform of the Virginia militia.

The pleasant life that Washington enjoyed at Mount Vernon with his beloved Martha was brought to an end when the news from Lexington and Concord swept the colonies. (Above, General Israel Putnam receives the news while ploughing a field.) In May, 1775, less than a month after the battle, Washington went to Philadelphia to attend the Second Continental Congress, held in Independence Hall. The scene that took place there on June 15 is depicted below.

In the chair, far left, sits John Hancock, President of the Congress. Standing in the middle of the room is John Adams about to propose Colonel Washington for commander in chief of the Continental armies. As Washington, far right, realizes that his name is before the Congress, he rises and slips out of the room so that the delegates can discuss him freely.

About noon they filed out of the hall and found Washington. Seizing his hand, they showered him with congratulations, and for the first time he heard himself addressed as "General."

When Washington assumed command of the army on July 3, 1775, at Cambridge, Massachusetts (above) there were sixteen thousand Americans camped in a semicircle around Boston. Most of them were farmers and town boys who had gathered of their own free will to drive the hated British out of Boston. They were raw and undisciplined. "They regarded an officer no more than a broomstick," said Washington. The loosely united colonies had no military tradition, few military stores, almost no industry and had no fleet or allies. At their backs were the hostile Iroquois. To the north was Canada, aligned with Britain, and within the colonies were countless American loyalists. Opposing them were the trained regulars of powerful England, backed by the world's greatest navy. It did not seem possible that America could win against such odds. But Washington never faltered.

His indomitable character rather than his sword won the American Revolution. The illustration (below) shows Washington studying battle plans for the coming day.

For over a year Washington's army suffered a series of defeats and was almost constantly on the run.

His first victory came on Christmas Eve, 1776, when he surprised and captured one thousand Hessians at Trenton. A few days later at Princeton (above) he rallied his faltering troops to win another battle. The country was electrified by the news.

At the left is Washington's camp chest which he carried throughout the Revolution. Its compartments were so ingeniously arranged that it held enough plates, cutlery, cooking utensils, flasks and food containers to serve a complete dinner for four.

On the opposite page is his first full-length portrait. It was painted by C. W. Peale and the scene is the Battle of Princeton. Note Washington's large hands and feet, and his youthful features.

After more than five years of war, during which Washington did not win a major battle, British General Cornwallis' army of seven thousand was entrenched on a narrow peninsula between the York and James rivers. A large French fleet was off- shore blocking his escape. With sixteen thousand French and Continental soldiers, Washington moved to the peninsula and the siege of Yorktown began. On October 9, 1781, the General himself fired the first gun (above).

For nine days the American and French batteries hammered incessantly at the British forces. Outnumbered, unable to escape by land or water, and with many of his men wounded and sick with smallpox, Cornwallis could find no way out. On October 17 he sent out a flag asking for terms (right). Two days later the formal surrender took place. The British, with shouldered arms, colors cased and drums beating, marched between two lines formed by the victorious army, which stretched out more than a mile in length. The British marched to the then popular tune of "The World Turned Upside Down"—a fitting number. They were led by General O'Hara on horseback, who rode up to Washington, took off his hat and apologized for the absence of the indisposed Cornwallis. Washington pointed to General Benjamin Lincoln

as the officer who was to receive the sword. (The Currier print below erroneously shows Cornwallis handing over the sword.) Although New York, Charleston and Savannah were still in the hands of the enemy, the surrender at Yorktown meant the virtual end of the war.

The real face of Washington is seen in this life mask.

14

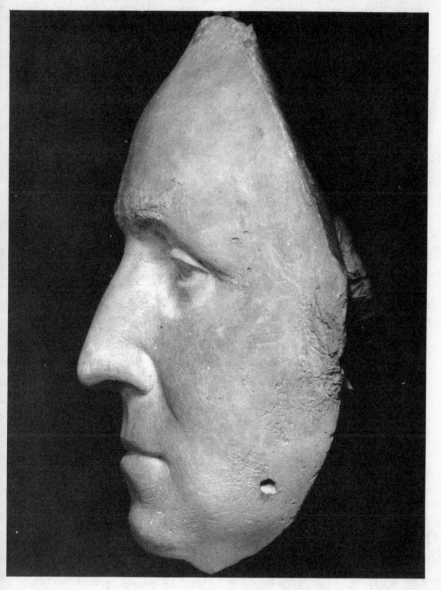

It was made by the French sculptor, Houdon, when Washington was fifty-three.

Washington had served his country without pay, save for actual expenses in the field, and now in 1783 after eight years of absence from Mount Vernon he was back home again, hoping to build up his neglected farm and live out his days. But the country had other plans for him. On April 14, 1789, Charles Thomson, Secretary of Congress, arrived in Mount Vernon and handed the General a dispatch notifying him of his unanimous election to the Presidency (above). Two days later he left for New York.

It was roses all the way for George —roses and triumphal arches and wreaths strewn in his path and wildly cheering people in every town through which he passed. At Trenton (left) he passed beneath an arch supported by thirteen columns in front of which were thirteen young girls dressed in white flowing robes. They sang, "Welcome, mighty Chief, once more . . ."

When he reached Elizabethtown, New Jersey, an elaborate barge, manned by thirteen sailing captains dressed in white uniforms, took him across the Hudson River and landed him at the foot of Wall Street.

Above, the General is about to mount the "elegant steps with their sides covered and carpeted" while Governor Clinton stands ready to greet him.

The inauguration of the first President of the United States took place on the afternoon of April 30, 1789, on the balcony of Federal Hall, which overlooked Broad and Wall streets. As Washington came out on the balcony he got a thunderous ovation from the people who jammed the streets and housetops as far as anyone could see. Then, as he took the oath of office in his dark brown American-made suit, a deep silence swept over the crowd. There was not a sound from the streets until Chancellor Robert R. Livingston, who administered the oath, stepped forward to the railing and shouted, "Long live George Washington, President of the United States." Again the crowd broke into cheers. The Stars and Stripes were raised on the staff above the balcony, and from the harbor a thirteen-gun salute announced the birth of a new republic.

Washington's cream-colored, English-made coach (below) was the best of its kind. Heavy and substantial, it was drawn by four, or sometimes six bay horses.

The first presidential mansion (above) was too small for Washington's ménage which consisted of his wife, her two grandchildren, four secretaries and a retinue of servants.

War; Thomas Jefferson, Secretary of State; Edmund Randolph (with back turned), Attorney General; Alexander Hamilton, Secretary of the Treasury. On the far right is the President, attired formally in a black velvet suit.

In May, 1789, when Martha arrived in New York, the Washingtons established a social routine which they pursued until they moved to Philadelphia the following year. Tuesday afternoons the President would receive callers and on Thursday nights state dinners would be held. The most sought-after invitation was one to Martha's formal receptions, held every Friday night (below).

Although Washington dreaded making appointments to office, he selected for his first Cabinet (as shown in this picture, from left to right): Henry Knox, Secretary of

The pomp and ceremony of the Administration was ridiculed by many people who did not like such things as the elaborate formality of Martha's receptions or the sight of the President being drawn about in his cream-colored carriage emblazoned with his coat of arms. It was too fancy, this "Republican Court" of the Monocrats, as they called the new Administration. Meanwhile the Senate debated whether the official presidential title should be "His Highness the President of the United States of America and Protector of their Liberties," or more simply "His Patriotic Majesty."

Washington himself was not immune from personal attacks. John Adams called him "an old mutton head" and Thomas Paine said that he was a hypocrite in public life. A few derisive cartoons were directed at him. One, entitled "The Entry," which appeared upon his arrival in New York, showed him riding upon an ass, supported by his Negro man-servant Billy, and is described as being "full of disloyal and profane allusions." Above is a rare caricature of Washington which was published in England while he was president.

WHEN WASHINGTON WAS PRESIDENT: The first successful balloon flight in America took place (left) when Jean Pierre Blanchard took off from Philadelphia on January 9, 1793 and landed forty minutes later in a New Jersey town about fifteen miles away. The flight was witnessed by Washington and other officials.

When the distilling farmers of western Pennsylvania refused to pay the excise tax on their product in 1794, Washington called out the militia of four states and went to Cumberland, Maryland, to review a force of 3,200 (below). The show of arms ended the Whiskey Rebellion. There was no bloodshed.

One of the most significant and far-reaching events that took place while Washington was president was the invention of the cotton gin by Eli Whitney in 1793. A young New Englander who had graduated from Yale the year before, Whitney went to Georgia expecting to teach school, when friends, aware of his mechanical ability, asked him if he could produce a machine that would clean cotton. The result was the gin which, within a decade, made cotton the cornerstone of the South's economic foundation.

A group of brokers trading under a buttonwood tree on Wall Street in 1792 signed an agreement which founded the New York Stock Exchange.

The President had a box and gave many theater parties in the John Street Theater, New York, which flourished from 1785 to 1798.

In March, 1797, at the end of his second term, Washington came home to Mount Vernon, arriving for the second time after an eight-year absence in the service of his country. "Grandpapa is very happy to be once more Farmer Washington," wrote Nellie Custis, Martha's granddaughter. He was content, as he said in his *Writings,* "To make, and sell, a little flour . . . To repair houses going fast to ruin . . . To amuse myself in agriculture and rural pursuits . . . Now and then to meet friends I esteem . . . would fill the measure and add zest to my enjoyments." With less than three years of life remaining, the enjoyments of Mount Vernon were not his for long.

Left, the silhouette made by his niece, Patty Custis, in his later years.

THE DEATH of GENERAL WASHINGTON

This most illustrious and much lamented Personage died on the 15th of Decr 1799, in the 68th year of his Age, after a short illness of 30 hours in the full Possession of all his Fame, like a Christian and an Hero, calm and collected, without a groan and without a sigh.

He united and adorned many excellent Characters, at once the Patriot and Politician, the Soldier & the Citizen, the Husbandman and the Hero, the Favourite of the Genius of Liberty, the Father of AMERICAN INDE-PENDENCE, the Promoter of her extensive and BROTHERLY UNION, the Pillar of her CON-STITUTION, the PRESIDENT of her SENATE; and the GENERALISSIMO of her ARMIES.

He possessed and displayed extraordinary abi-lities, exalted VIRTUES, and unexampled Self command and Self denial; moderate in Prosperity, undaunted amid Danger, unbroken by adversity, firm and unmoved amid the violence & reproach of Faction, unperverted by great and general applause.

He Was GREAT in the COUNCIL, and in the FIELD.

He Was GREAT in ARTS, and in ARMS.

First in War, first in Peace, first in the hearts of AMERICANS, first in the Eyes of the World, he was unrivalled as a Statesman as a Soldier, as a Senator: and he is embalmed by the tears of AMERICA, entombed in the hearts of his Countrymen, admired by the enlightened of all Lands, immortalized by his own great actions and the regrets of Mankind.

The doctors took about a quart of blood out of Washington as he lay ill with a high fever and a sore throat. Shortly afterward he said, "I find I am going." Toward evening he murmured, "I die hard but I am not afraid to go." Then, to the three doctors in attendance, he spoke his final words: "I thank you for your attention, you had better not take any more trouble about me, but let me go off quietly." He died, accord-ing to his secretary, Tobias Lear, "With perfect resignation, and in full possession of his reason . . ." Death came to the General on December 14, 1799. He was buried in the family tomb at Mount Vernon (below).

JOHN ADAMS 1735–1826
President 1797–1801

John Adams was not a happy president. It was not in his irritable nature to be very happy anyway and he had less reason to be so during his political career. As vice-president under Washington for eight years he was completely overshadowed by the stately and heroic President. (Adams was short, chubby, wore plain clothes, and was called "His Rotundity" behind his back.) When he was inaugurated on March 4, 1797, at Philadelphia, he still played second fiddle to Washington. On what should have been the greatest day of his life the cheers of the crowd were all for the retiring President. They forgot about the little man who was being sworn in. Bitterly he wrote his wife: "He [Washington] seemed to enjoy a triumph over me. Methought I heard him say: 'Ay! I am fairly out, and you fairly in! See which one of us will be the happiest!' " Like Washington and Alexander Hamilton, Adams was a Federalist, the party that represented the old Colonial aristocracy. It was not a popular party and died four years later when Adams was defeated by Thomas Jefferson, his own Vice-President.

In the plain house on the right (above), which is still standing in Quincy, Massachusetts, John was born on October 30, 1735. His father was a small farmer and the village cobbler. At fifteen, John entered Harvard where at that time the college catalogue rated students according to social standing. John ranked fourteen in a class of twenty-four. Upon graduation he went to Worcester where he taught school and studied law for two years, then came home to work as a part-time farmer and lawyer. Adams quickly rose from obscurity when he presented resolutions opposing the Stamp Act in 1765. So clearly did he present the people's case as an invasion of their rights by Britain that his resolutions were immediately adopted throughout the colony. Although a dedicated patriot to the American cause, he had enough courage to defend the British Captain, Thomas Preston, charged with murder in the Boston Massacre. Adams was respected, though never popular. The people of Massachusetts sent him to the First Continental Congress in 1774. He helped draft the Declaration of Independence and during the Revolution he was commissioner to France and minister to Holland.

The Adams homes in Quincy (opposite page), which were built about 1675, were bought by the second President's father and remained in possession of his descendants until 1940 when they were deeded to the city of Quincy. John, as noted, was born in the house on the right—known as the cottage. Upon the death of his father in 1761, John inherited the other house, where his son John Quincy Adams, the sixth President, was born in 1767. Restored and repaired, the two birthplaces contain many of the original furnishings and are now national shrines.

Among the American Peace Commissioners who signed the Treaty of Paris in 1783 (below) to end the Revolution were John Adams (seated, left); John Jay, America's first Chief Justice of the Supreme Court (extreme left); and Benjamin Franklin (center).

Artist Benjamin West was unable to finish this painting because the British Commissioner died before its completion without leaving a likeness of himself for West to copy.

Abigail Smith Adams, a witty and attractive woman, married John in 1764. She was the wife of one president and the mother of another, and the first American to be presented at the Court of St. James.

John Adams outlived Abigail by eight years and lived to see his son installed in the White House. He died on the fiftieth Fourth of July (1826), on the same day that Thomas Jefferson breathed his last.

The winning design in a competition open to architects for "The President's House" (above) was submitted by James Hoban, an Irishman. His design followed the exterior of the Duke of Leinster's Palace in Dublin. The cornerstone was laid on October 13, 1792, and it was the first public building erected in Washington. Hoban supervised its construction and was criticized because of its cost ($400,000) and its size, "big enough," said Thomas Jefferson, "for two emperors, one Pope and the Grand Lama." That might have been sour grapes, however, for Jefferson submitted a design and came out second. John and Abigail moved in eight years after the cornerstone was laid. The house stood on a desolate bog. There were no bathrooms and water had to be carried by hand from a distance of five city blocks. "We had not the least fence, yard or other conveniences without," wrote Abigail, "and the great unfinished audience room, I made a drying room of." There were no stairs inside or out and no call bells "to assist us in this great castle."

BUILDING THE FIRST WHITE HOUSE

WHEN JOHN ADAMS WAS PRESIDENT: The United States Capitol (right) looked like this, Washington had a population of 3,210, the nation itself about five million, and the road between Philadelphia and Washington passed through such a wilderness that John and Abigail got lost on the way.

In an undeclared shooting war with France that lasted two and a half years, the American Navy took eighty-five French ships and lost only one. Left, the American frigate *Constellation* forces *L'Insurgente* to surrender, February 9, 1799. The trouble began when France and England were at war and both countries seized American ships at will.

A phenomenon of the Adams Administration was the Great Revival that swept the western frontier of America, then Kentucky and Tennessee. Without enough ministers to serve them, great crowds thronged to "sacramental meetings" and listened to the exhortations of the revivalists. Often the meetings were accompanied by bodily exercises such as falling to the ground, weeping, shouting, barking, leaping and dancing. An example of the exercises is shown, right.

31

THOMAS JEFFERSON 1743–1826
President 1801–1809

Thomas Jefferson was the first president to be inaugurated in Washington (March 4, 1801), and the first to be elected by the House of Representatives. This came about when Jefferson and Aaron Burr, leaders of the Democrat-Republicans, each received seventy-three electoral votes and the House broke the tie by electing Jefferson. According to the law then in operation, Burr, the second-highest candidate, became vice-president.

The tall, auburn-haired, sharp-featured Jefferson spoke for the masses —the farmers, pioneers and apprentices—and despised what he called "the aristocracy of wealth." Yet he was an aristocrat to his finger tips. He owned some two hundred slaves, a large plantation, and the grandest house in Virginia.

In the White House his staff of fourteen servants included a French chef, and his dinner parties were frequent and lavish. At the same time he cut out many glittering presidential ceremonials, opened his doors to all without regard to social classification, came and went like any other citizen and often did his own marketing.

A many-sided and perplexing man was Jefferson. He was at once a musician, an architect, inventor, philosopher, statesman, brilliant lawyer and talented writer. He was, too, a revolutionist, an idealist and a sincere believer in the rights of man. It was only natural that such a many-sided man should be seen in many different ways. Some saw him as a near god; others saw him as did his political enemy, Alexander Hamilton, who said that he was a "concealed voluptuary . . . in the plain garb of Quaker simplicity."

WHEN JEFFERSON WAS PRESIDENT: Robert Fulton launched the first successful steamboat (above). Christened "The North River Steamboat of Clermont" but popularly called the *Clermont,* Fulton's craft plied between New York and Albany in 1807, carrying up to ninety passengers a trip at seven dollars a head. Although he did not invent the steamboat, he was the first man to assemble working parts that made it a commercial success.

The subject of many American legends is the wandering pioneer, Johnny Appleseed (left), who ranged widely throughout the Ohio Valley planting apple seeds and pruning growing trees from 1800 until his death in 1845. He was a real person named John Chapman, born in New England about 1774. His sole purpose in life was to encourage the growth of apples along the western frontier. He is celebrated in literature in Vachel Lindsay's "In Praise of Johnny Appleseed."

34

The greatest event of the Jefferson regime was the purchase of the Louisiana Territory from Napoleon. For fifteen million dollars the area of our country was more than doubled in size—the greatest peacetime acquisition of land in the history of any nation. The ceremonial transfer took place in New Orleans (above) on December 20, 1803, when the Tricolor of France was hauled down and the American flag was raised in its place.

When Alexander Hamilton, the political foe and outspoken critic of Aaron Burr, was killed in a duel by the Vice-President on June 11, 1804, the nation was shocked and angered. Although Burr had killed his man fairly and dueling was not illegal, it was the end of Burr's political career. He finished his term as vice-president but was dropped from the ticket by the Republicans. Later he attempted to rouse the western states to secede and was tried for treason. He was acquitted but became an outcast.

The demands for tribute and the cruelty of the Barbary pirates caused Jefferson to curb them by naval action. As an example of their cruelty (right) the pirates return the French consul to his ship via cannon.

Jefferson spent twenty-five years on and off building his dream house, Monticello (little mountain), on a hilltop overlooking Charlottesville. It was here that he brought his bride, the twenty-four-year-old widow Martha Wayles Skelton, in 1772. (Ten years later as she lay dying he promised her that he would never remarry, and he never did.) From Monticello, Jefferson was forced to dash off on horseback to escape the invading British in 1781 when he was governor of Virginia.

All the materials that went into the construction of Monticello, even the bricks, were made on the place by Jefferson's slaves. His inventiveness is shown in the pictures below. Lower left: a fireplace containing a dumb-waiter. Below: an alcove bedroom between separate dressing rooms.

Jefferson left the White House at the end of his second term without regret and retired to Monticello where he spent the rest of his life. A voluminous letter writer, he answered by hand the flood of letters that came to him on the above chair-desk of his own making. Jefferson died in virtual poverty and the house with all its furnishings was sold to satisfy his creditors. For many years Monticello was unoccupied and fell into near ruins (below). Fortunately it was later restored.

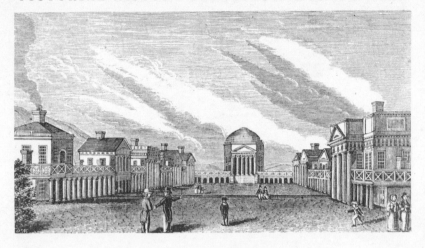

On a terrace behind his house Jefferson installed a telescope and would daily peer through it to watch in the valley below the red brick structures of the University of Virginia (above) rising up year after year. Jefferson raised the money for the construction, designed the buildings and selected the faculty. The founding of the University was one of his fondest dreams. He valued it so highly that it was one of the three achievements in his life that he thought worthy of mention on his tombstone: the Declaration of Independence, the Statute of Religious Freedom for the State of Virginia, and the University. In this self-made tribute he did not mention that he was governor of Virginia, envoy, vice-president, president, or that he added an empire to the United States by the Louisiana Purchase.

Below is the desk on which he wrote the Declaration of Independence. Opposite page: the rough draft of a page of the Declaration, in his handwriting.

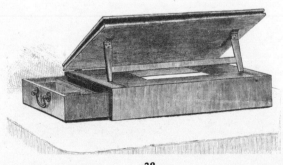

A Declaration by the Representatives of the UNITED STATES
OF AMERICA, in General Congress assembled.

When in the course of human events it becomes necessary for one people to
dissolve the political bands which have connected them with another, and to as-
-sume among the powers of the earth the separate and equal station to
which the laws of nature & of nature's god entitle them, a decent respect
to the opinions of mankind requires that they should declare the causes
which impel them to the separation.

We hold these truths to be self-evident; that all men are
created equal, that they are endowed by their creator with equal
rights, that among these are life, liberty, & the pursuit of happiness; that to secure these, go-
-vernments are instituted among men, deriving their just powers from
the consent of the governed; that whenever any form of government
becomes destructive of these ends, it is the right of the people to alter
or to abolish it, & to institute new government, laying it's foundation on
such principles & organising it's powers in such form, as to them shall
seem most likely to effect their safety & happiness. prudence indeed
will dictate that governments long established should not be changed for
light & transient causes: and accordingly all experience hath shewn that
mankind are more disposed to suffer while evils are sufferable, than to
right themselves by abolishing the forms to which they are accustomed. but
when a long train of abuses & usurpations [begun at a distinguished period,
&] pursuing invariably the same object, evinces a design to reduce
them under absolute despotism, it is their right, it is their duty, to throw off such
government & to provide new guards for their future security. such has
been the patient sufferance of these colonies; & such is now the necessity
which constrains them to expunge their former systems of government.
the history of the present king of Great Britain is a history of unremitting injuries and
usurpations [among which appears no solitary fact to contra-
-dict the uniform tenor of the rest all of which have in direct object the
establishment of an absolute tyranny over these states. to prove this, let facts be
submitted to a candid world [for the truth of which we pledge a faith
yet unsullied by falsehood]

JAMES MADISON 1751–1836
President 1809–1817

"Mrs. Madison is a fine, portly, buxom dame, who has a smile and a pleasant word for everybody . . . but as for Jemmy Madison—ah! poor Jemmy! He is but a withered little apple-John." Thus did Washington Irving describe the President and his lady in a letter written in 1811. An apple-John is an apple considered to be in perfection only when it is withered and shriveled, and the President fitted the description. He was our smallest president, standing only five feet, four inches and weighing about one hundred pounds. An unprepossessing figure—more of a mind than a man—he had a tiny, almost inaudible voice, but he was gentle, kind and scholarly. A Virginian and a Princeton graduate (class of 1772), Madison served his country well as the "Father of the Constitution," champion of the Bill of Rights (the first ten amendments), member of Congress and secretary of state under Jefferson for eight years. Although he lacked executive ability, Madison was a "great little man," to quote Aaron Burr who, incidentally, introduced him to his future wife,

Dolly Payne Todd (above), the widowed daughter of a Philadelphia boardinghouse-keeper.

Had it not been for Dolly, her husband's regime would have been a dull one, but she was as flamboyant and colorful as he was drab. She was the first urbane-minded woman to dwell in the White House. She was endowed with the social touch, gave brilliant parties and dressed the part. Her trade-mark was the bejeweled and feathered turbans which matched her Parisian dresses, and cost her one thousand dollars a year. Much to the disgust of some ladies who remembered her humble Quaker origin, she dipped snuff and used rouge and lipstick. Warmhearted and lively, she ruled her court with charm and had a rare memory for names and faces. She had great tact too, for she lived in harmony under the same roof with her mother-in-law for many years.

Madison was twenty-one years older than Dolly and shorter by a head. He was reserved, dignified and precise. She was cordial, gay and amiable. Despite their different natures they were devoted to each other all their lives. Dolly referred to the President with real affection as "my darling little husband."

41

One of the few bright spots in "Mr. Madison's War," as the War of 1812 was often called, was the defeat of England's *Guerrière* by the *Constitution* (above).

The day the British burned Washington was one of the most disgraceful days in American history. Admiral Sir George Cockburn, who had previously burned and pillaged Havre de Grace, Maryland (left), led a British expeditionary force of about five thousand into Washington on August 24, 1814, and put the torch to the Capitol, the White House and most every other public building. Had it not been for a sudden downpour, the entire city would have been burned to the ground. The unprepared and loosely organized American troops fled to the hills of Georgetown before the invading British. Madison himself was a refugee in the hills and got miserably drenched in the downpour. Dolly, too, had to run for it, but before leaving the White House she hurriedly grabbed everything of value she could. Among the things she had packed into a waiting cart was a Stuart portrait of Washington which she had removed from its frame so that it could be more easily carried off.

Two days later Dolly returned to the White House (above) and found it a fire-swept, uninhabitable ruin with only the four walls standing. The portrait she saved (below) now hangs in the East Room.

In September, 1814, the Madisons moved into the Octagon House (below). They never again occupied the White House, as repairs were not completed until 1817, by which time Monroe was president.

The final victory of the War of 1812 was the Battle of New Orleans which took place on January 8, 1815, two weeks after the war was over. (The news of the Treaty of Ghent signed with England on Christmas Eve, 1814, did not reach America until after the battle had been fought.) The picture above, as seen from the British lines, shows the British regulars advancing as though on parade in a direct assault on General Andrew Jackson's entrenched Tennessee and Kentucky riflemen. The result was an unbelievable slaughter. In less than a half hour seven hundred British were killed, fourteen hundred wounded, and five hundred captured. The American loss was eight killed, thirteen wounded.

The Treaty of Ghent was simply an end to hostilities and a return to the prewar status. The impressment of American seamen—the main issue of the war—was not mentioned, but England tacitly agreed to discontinue the practice. This picture of the Treaty (left) shows the British representative Admiral Lord Gambier shaking hands with John Quincy Adams, America's Chief Plenipotentiary.

WHEN MADISON WAS PRESI-
DENT: A surgeon named Ephraim
McDowell made medical history by
performing the first ovariotomy, at
Danville, Kentucky, on Christmas
Day, 1809 (right). He removed a
twenty-two-and-one-half-pound ovar-
ian tumor from Mrs. Jane Crawford, forty-seven, who endured the
half-hour-long operation without an
anaesthetic. In twenty-five days she
returned on horseback fully recovered to her home sixty miles from
Danville. Today McDowell is honored as the "Founder of Abdominal
Surgery."

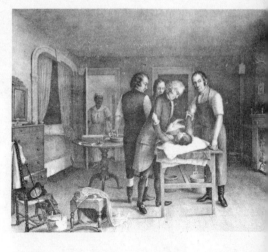

America's first champion was Tom
Molyneux (below) who went to England in 1810 and twice fought the
British champion, Tom Cribb. Molyneux got tricked out of victory in the
first fight, lost the second fairly.

Among the first American authors
to be read abroad was Washington
Irving, shown above with the character of his invention, Diedrich
Knickerbocker.

JAMES MONROE 1758–1831
President 1817–1825

James Monroe, a lanky, blue-eyed, commonplace man of no great brilliance, was the last of the Virginia Dynasty (Jefferson, Madison and Monroe) which dominated American politics for a quarter of a century, the last president to be elected with virtually no opposition, and the last to wear knee breeches. His first administration was so serene and successful that when he ran for office the second time (1820) he received 231 out of 232 electoral votes. His harmonious eight-year administration covered what is known as "The Era of Good Feeling." America had a lot to feel good about. Even the hard-core Federalists, so long opposed to the Virginia Dynasty, had to give credit to Monroe's constructive statesmanship. Among his achievements were the purchase of Florida from Spain, the United States-Great Britain agreement which pledged the two countries to disarm themselves forever along the Canadian border, and the Missouri Compromise which admitted Missouri as a slave state but prohibited further slavery above the Mason-Dixon Line, thus binding the North and South together. His greatest triumph was the Monroe Doctrine which announced to the world that the American continents "are henceforth not to be considered as subjects for future colonization by any European powers."

Elizabeth Kortright Monroe (above) was a stately, regal woman whose White House receptions were noted for their stiff formality in contrast to those of her predecessor, Dolly Madison.

Below, a page of the Monroe Doctrine in the President's handwriting, from the message to Congress, December 2, 1823.

WHEN MONROE WAS PRESIDENT: Major S. H. Long made a two-year scientific exploration of the Great Plains and reported that the area was "almost wholly unfit for cultivation." The report was ignored by a great number of people who pushed west across the Alleghenies (left) in the decade following the opening of the first link of the Cumberland Road in 1815. The road was eventually extended from Cumberland, Maryland, the head of navigation on the Potomac, to Vandalia, Illinois.

A typical New York street scene of the 1820s is shown right, in the days when pigs, cattle, dogs and chickens ran loose in the unpaved streets to the discomfiture of pedestrians. Here, a fair one gets dumped by a strolling pig.

The Monroe administration saw an agrarian awakening which resulted in the growth of county and state fairs. This painting (left) is entitled "The County Fair, 1824."

In 1819 the *Savannah* (right), equipped with steam engine and paddle wheels, sailed out of Savannah, Georgia, and made Liverpool twenty-nine days later, arriving there on June 20. To the *Savannah* goes the honor of being the first steamship to cross the Atlantic even though she used more sail than steam during the voyage. Coming into Liverpool she let out so much smoke that a British cruiser hastened to her rescue, thinking she was on fire.

In 1823 James Fenimore Cooper published *The Pioneers,* the first of his world-famous *Leatherstocking Tales.* He was the first American author whose works were widely translated in Europe. The scene (left) is from *The Pioneers.*

In the 1820s the theater, like most everything else in America, enjoyed a period of prosperity. This picture (right) shows New York's glittering Park Theater which opened on September 1, 1821, before 2,500 people.

JOHN QUINCY ADAMS 1767–1848
President 1825–1829

John Quincy Adams and his father had much in common. To begin with, they were born in houses standing right next to each other on the same plot of land (see page 27), and were both rocked in the same cradle (above). Both went to Harvard, became lawyers, served as ministers to Holland and England, and as president (for one term only). In Quincy their graves, like their birthplaces, are side by side. Physically they had much in common, both being chubby and bald.

Young John Quincy (the *c* is pronounced as *z*) was a world traveler long before he entered Harvard. When he was ten his father took him to France and by the time he was twelve he had crossed the ocean four times. On one trip they were shipwrecked off Spain and spent three months on the road getting to Paris. At fourteen, in 1781, the bright youngster was in St. Petersburg serving as private secretary and interpreter to Francis Dana, the American Minister to Russia. Two years later he was the United States secretary at the Treaty of Paris which ended the American Revolution. No president has ever served his country so long or in so many capacities: minister to Holland, Berlin, Russia and England, United States senator, secretary of state, peace commissioner, president, and in the last eighteen years of his life (1831–1848), a member of Congress.

John Quincy Adams was our only nonpartisan president and the first to receive fewer popular and electoral votes than an opponent. This came about due to the peculiar system then in use. In the 1824 election there were four candidates, all Democrat-Republicans. Andrew Jackson received 153,544 popular and 99 electoral votes; Adams polled 108,740 popular and 84 electoral votes; William Harris Crawford and Henry Clay received 42 and 37 electoral votes respectively. Since no candidate had a majority of the electoral votes it devolved upon the House of Representatives to choose from the highest three. The House elected Adams when Clay, who did not want to see Jackson president, released his votes to Adams. Jackson was livid. Adams was unhappy because he knew that he was not the popular choice. Clay was made secretary of state. The followers of Adams and Clay called themselves National Republicans and later merged into the Whigs.

The icy-veined Adams led a Spartan life in the White House. He rose at five, read the Bible and took a walk or a swim in the Potomac. One

morning while swimming, someone stole his clothes, and he had to appeal to a boy to run up to the White House to get another suit. The lad must have been startled at the sight of the nude, pink-domed President pacing the bank. Another of his diversions was billiards. When the news was made public that he had installed a billiard table in the White House and had billed the government for "billiard table $50; cues $5; billiard balls $6" he was roundly denounced as a profligate. He paid the government back out of his own pocket.

On January 8, 1824, on the occasion of the anniversary of the Battle of New Orleans, a ball was given by the Adamses in honor of General Jackson, which outshone any function given by the Monroes, then in the White House. About one thousand people attended, among whom were (above, left to right) John C. Calhoun, Daniel Webster, General Jackson, Henry Clay and Adams, the President-to-be. The Washington *Republican* described the elaborate ball in a long five-stanza poem, each stanza ending with:

Belles and matrons, maids and madams
All are gone to Mrs. Adams'.

Louisa Catherine Johnson, daughter of the American Consul in London, married John Quincy Adams in England on July 26, 1797. This portrait was painted by Gilbert Stuart in 1818 when she was forty-three.

WHEN JOHN QUINCY ADAMS WAS PRESIDENT: Governor De Witt Clinton of New York inaugurated the opening of the 363-mile-long Erie Canal by pouring a cask of Lake Erie water into the sea to symbolize the "marriage of the waters." The event (left) took place in New York Bay on November 4, 1825, and was hailed throughout the country as a great victory.

America's first horse-drawn railway was built in 1826 at Quincy, Massachusetts, and was used to draw stone from a quarry.

Noah Webster (below) published his first complete dictionary in 1828. It contained more definitions than any previous work.

In 1827 Joseph Smith (above) said that the Angel Moroni appeared before him at Palmyra, New York, and delivered the plates of a book, telling him to start a new religious sect. The revelation led to the founding of the Church of Jesus Christ of Latter-Day Saints whose followers are the Mormons.

The young and expanding country had little time for organized sports when Adams was president. There were some horse racing, football (soccer), cricket, town ball (the forerunner of baseball), cockfighting and an occasional, though illegal, bareknuckle prize fight. The sport of archery was one of the first to be organized in this country when, in 1828, a group of twenty-five young gentlemen formed the United Bowmen of Philadelphia (right). For thirty years the club conducted matches and tournaments for silver trophies. Other clubs followed suit, and in 1879 the first National Archery Tournament was held at White Stocking Park, Chicago.

For many years coal was regarded as a black stone and was used only by a few blacksmiths in their forges. When it was found that it made a good heating fuel it was mined commercially. Below, a primitive mine in Wheeling, Virginia, about 1825.

This is the Capitol as Adams saw it, after it had been rebuilt by Charles Bulfinch and Benjamin Latrobe. The four rows of poplar trees were planted by Thomas Jefferson in 1801. The brown dome was replaced during Lincoln's administration.

Above: John Quincy Adams at sixteen. Above, right: as he looked in 1795, aged twenty-eight. Below, left: a silhouette cut in the White House. Below, right: a bust made from a life mask when he was fifty-eight.

The boy who saw the Battle of Bunker Hill (from a hilltop near his home) lived long enough to be photographed. The daguerreotype, right, was made in 1847 when he was seventy-nine, the year before he died.

After he left the White House he retired to Quincy for two years, then came back into public life as a congressman. The political comedown never bothered him nor did he ever seek any special consideration because of the high office he once held. He was too busy fighting the gag rule which the House adopted to prevent the introduction of antislavery petitions. Outraged that the people could no longer be heard through their representatives, Adams alone fought the measure year after year until finally, in 1844, it was repealed. Four years later he suddenly collapsed on the floor of the House and was carried to a bed set up for him in the Speaker's office (right). For two days he lingered; then died, still at his post in the Capitol.

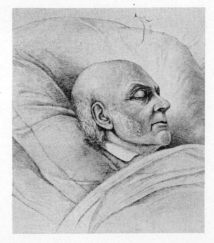

ANDREW JACKSON 1767–1845
President 1829–1837

Andrew Jackson was a true son of the frontier, the first president born in a log cabin (above), and the first who was not of the Virginia aristocracy or a Massachusetts Adams. A tall, lean, poorly educated backwoodsman with a crest of hair almost red and a temper in keeping, he was a reckless horseman, cockfighter and duelist. No two presidents ever presented a sharper contrast than the suave, cultured John Quincy Adams and the man who followed him. As a boy, when young Adams at the same age was secretary and interpreter for our minister to Russia, Andy scratched out a memorandum in his notebook which serves to illustrate the difference between the two. "How to feed a cock before you him fight Take and give him some Pickle Beaf Cut fine . . ." he wrote. Years later when Harvard College conferred upon President Jackson a degree of Doctor of Laws, Adams was horrified. Was there no way to prevent this outrage, he asked the president of Harvard. "None," was the answer. "As the people have twice decided that this man knows law enough to be their ruler it is not for Harvard College to maintain that they are mistaken."

Jackson was by no means the "barbarian who could not write a sentence of grammar and hardly could spell his own name" that Adams said he was. He was courtly, gracious and dignified when the occasion demanded—as well mannered as any president.

Jackson earned his nickname of Old Hickory during the War of 1812 in his campaign against the Creek Indians of Alabama. Leading a ragged, ill-provisioned army, he slept on the ground with his men and ate the same slim rations. "He's tough as hickory," his admiring troops said, and the name stuck.

He had to be as tough as hickory to survive, for he was born and lived in a hard world. His father, also named Andrew, was a tenant farmer of North Ireland who migrated to this country in 1765 with his wife and two sons. The family settled in the wilderness of North Carolina, and had lived there only two years when the father died. His destitute widow, Elizabeth, took refuge with a sister in Waxhaw, South Carolina, where Andy was born on March 15, 1767, a few weeks after the death of his father.

In 1780 when Andy was thirteen, he attached himself to an American encampment, and served as a mounted messenger for more than a year when he was captured with his brother, Robert, by a body of British dragoons. While the British wrecked the house in which he was held, the officer in command "in very imperious tones" commanded Andy to clean his boots. When he refused, the officer struck him a violent blow with his sword which cut the boy's upraised hand to the bone and crashed on his head, leaving a scar that he carried for life (above). While prisoners, the boys contracted smallpox and were released. Shortly afterward Robert died and was soon followed by the mother. Hugh, the oldest brother, had died the year before and now Andy at fourteen was alone in the world.

The rugged youth had many adventures in the wilderness. Once he was pulled ashore just as he was about to go over a cataract on a raft (left).

Andrew grew up as wild as the frontier itself and became notorious for his tavern brawls and gambling on cockfights and horse races. An early biography describes him when he was eighteen and living in Salisbury, North Carolina as ". . . the most roaring, rollicking, game-cocking, horse-racing, card-playing, mischievous fellow, that ever lived in Salisbury . . . the head of the rowdies hereabouts." He found time, however, to study law and at the age of twenty was admitted to the North Carolina bar. The following year he crossed the mountains of the state into what is now Tennessee and set up a law office in Nashville.

Below is a miniature on ivory of Jackson, painted in New Orleans shortly after the battle in 1815, when he was forty-eight. It was done by Jean François Vallé, a Frenchman imbued with the Napoleonic tradition.

In Nashville, Jackson stayed at the boardinghouse of Mrs. John Donelson, whose attractive daughter Rachel soon caught his eye. Rachel was the estranged wife of Lewis Robards of Kentucky. Robards had started divorce proceedings, then dropped them without his wife's knowledge. Believing that the divorce had gone through, she married Jackson in 1791. Two years later the couple was startled to learn that no divorce had been granted and that Robards was now seeking one on the grounds of his wife's adultery. This time it was granted and Rachel and Jackson remarried. All her life Rachel was unjustly slandered for her too hasty second marriage.

Below, a reproduction of a miniature on ivory of Rachel when she was fifty-two. Jackson always wore this miniature next to his heart, suspended around his neck by a strong black cord. It was painted in 1819.

During the 1790s Jackson was the most successful lawyer in Nashville, and when Tennessee became a state in 1796 (the sixteenth to be admitted to the Union) he was elected as its first representative in Congress. Later he served as United States senator and justice of the Tennessee Supreme Court. His heart's desire was to live like a gentleman farmer in the Virginia tradition, and in 1804 he established the Hermitage plantation near Nashville as his residence. Remodeled and completed (left), it was the finest home in the state.

Fame knocked on Jackson's door in 1812 when he was given command of Tennessee troops to fight the Creek nation, allied to England. In one great battle at Horseshoe Bend (March 27, 1814) he destroyed the Indian power. Below, a Creek chief, Red Eagle, who was three-quarters white and was born William Weatherford, surrenders to Jackson.

Old Hickory avenged his scars at the Battle of New Orleans (above) and from that hour he was a national hero. In New Orleans church bells rang, cannons boomed and flowers were strewn in the path of the victorious troops. So popular was Jackson that when Judge Dominick Hall fined him one thousand dollars for arresting a civilian and placing him on trial before a court-martial, the people of New Orleans raised the amount and offered it to him. Jackson waved it aside, requesting that the money be given to the widows and orphans of the battle. He paid the fine out of his own pocket and rode out of town in glory. A successful campaign against the Seminole Indians in Florida (1817–1818) kept Jackson in the public eye. People began to talk of making him president.

Right, the statue of General Jackson, America's first equestrian monument, now located in Lafayette Park, Washington.

Some Account of some of the Bloody Deeds
OF
GENERAL JACKSON.

The campaign of 1828 was a battle of personalities between John Quincy Adams and Jackson and was marked by scurrilous abuse of the two leaders. An example was the Coffin Handbill broadside which depicted Jackson as a murderer because he had approved the execution of six mutineers during the War of 1812. Worse than that was the airing of Rachel's bigamy. Six weeks after the election Rachel came across a pamphlet recalling the old story, and though it was published in her defense she realized that the whole country knew about it. Distressed, she took to her bed and died—killed, so Jackson thought, by the lies of his political enemies. There was no joy in his heart as he drove from Tennessee to Washington (above) to take up solitary residence in the White House. He was sixty-two, grief-stricken and weary—probably the saddest man who ever entered the White House.

The mob that followed Jackson after the inaugural ceremonies at the Capitol swept into the White House and nearly took it apart (below). The pressure of the crowd was so great that women fainted, clothing was torn, glasses and china shattered. People stood on $150 official chairs to get a glimpse of the President. In danger of being mobbed, Jackson escaped by the back way and retreated to Gadsby's Hotel. Finally the crowd was lured outside when tubs of punch were placed on the lawn.

Another mob scene took place later in his administration when Jackson's admirers lugged a 1,400-pound cheese inside the White House and presented it to him. For hours a crowd of men, women and boys hacked at it (above), leaving only a small piece for the President.

WHEN JACKSON WAS PRESIDENT: The South Carolina Railroad put into service the first practical American-made locomotive, named "The Best Friend." After a few trial runs it made its first excursion trip (as shown above) on January 15, 1831. The engine's career ended a few weeks later when it exploded. In order to secure passengers after that, the railroad had to separate each locomotive from the cars with a flatcar loaded with bales of cotton. Jackson was the first president to ride on a railroad.

The junction of the Erie and Champlain canals (above) typified the growth of waterways during the Canal Era.

The Battle of Bad Axe (left) fought at the mouth of the Wisconsin river by that name on August 2, 1832, resulted in the defeat of Sac and Fox Indians by United States troops, and brought the Black Hawk War to an end. The Chief, Black Hawk, was captured and taken to Washington and presented to President Jackson. Abraham Lincoln and Jefferson Davis both served in the war.

A great fire swept New York City, December 16–17, 1835, and destroyed over six hundred buildings (above). Engines came from cities as far away as Philadelphia. Fires were the scourge of early American cities which were built largely of wood.

Cyrus Hall McCormick invented a successful reaping machine which was first demonstrated in 1831 and patented three years later. Large-scale production of the machine in Chicago resulted in the formation of the International Harvester Corporation.

In 1808 Congress enacted measures against the further introduction of slaves into the United States. This did not stop the practice, however. The illegal slave trade flourished right up to the Civil War as the picture below indicates: "A Slave Buyer in Africa, 1835."

Mrs. Frances Trollope.

Author of "The Domestic Manners of the Americans."

In 1832 English visitor Frances Trollope published a book ridiculing American life. This caricature, from the *Comic Almanac, 1834,* is how America saw *her.*

Peggy O'Neal Eaton (above) was a lively young woman of easy virtue (so everyone said) who set off an explosion in Washington social and political circles. The daughter of a tavern-keeper, Peggy married a naval officer, carried on an affair with John H. Eaton, Jackson's old friend, while her husband was at sea, then married her lover shortly after receiving the news of her first husband's death aboard ship. (Some said it was suicide.) This, and other flamboyant deeds in her past, did not sit well with Washington society even after her second husband was elevated to the position of secretary of war. The wives of the other Cabinet members refused to receive her. Emily Donelson, Jackson's niece who was hostess of the White House, would not talk to her. Jackson was furious, believing Peggy to be a victim of slander just as his Rachel had been. The President sent Emily off to Tennessee, called a Cabinet meeting and told the members that Peggy was "as chaste as a virgin," and that they had better think so or get out. They all did except Secretary of State Martin Van Buren who was a widower and had nothing to lose socially by recognizing Peggy.

"The Rats Leaving a Falling House" was the title of this 1831 cartoon (right) which shows the Cabinet members scurrying off with Van Buren held fast by Jackson's foot.

Jackson firmly believed in rule by the people and adopted the principle that "to the victor belongs the spoils." He fired 919 federal officeholders and gave their jobs to his friends and supporters. He hated all banks, particularly Nicholas Biddle's powerful Bank of the United States which controlled the government's finances. In 1832 when Biddle sought a new charter for his bank, Jackson vetoed the bill which Congress had passed for the purpose, and sealed the bank's doom. This cartoon (below) shows Major Jack Downing, a humorous character symbolizing the people, applauding Jackson while Biddle and his friends run for their lives amid the crashing pillars of the bank.

Jackson was equally bold when he put down the threatened revolt of South Carolina by sending armed forces to the state. Racked with tuberculosis most of the time he was president (he treated it by bleeding himself), Jackson died at the Hermitage in 1845, aged seventy-eight.

MARTIN VAN BUREN 1782–1862
President 1837–1841

"Little Van," hand-picked by Jackson to be his successor, was the first president who was not born a British subject, and the first of Dutch ancestry. Small, dapper and elegant in his manners and dress, he was completely unlike his flame-tempered predecessor. Van Buren was unassertive, amiable, and always courteous —and he dressed the part, as this description of him as he looked in 1828 while attending church indicates: "Mr. Van Buren was rather an exquisite in appearance. His complexion was a bright blond, and he dressed accordingly. He wore an elegant snuff-colored broadcloth coat with a velvet collar; his cravat was orange with modest lace tips; his vest was of a pearl hue; his trousers were white duck; his shoes were morocco; his neatly fitting gloves were yellow kid; his long-furred beaver hat with a broad brim was of a Quaker color."

Van Buren was born in Kinderhook, New York, a little village on the east bank of the Hudson. At fourteen he left school to study law and two years later astonished the people of his home town by winning his first lawsuit. A capable and wily politician, he went up the ladder step by step to fill the roles of state senator, attorney general of New York, United States senator, governor of New York, and under Jackson, secretary of state, minister to England and vice-president. So skilled was he in political manipulation that he earned a variety of nicknames, such as: the "Little Magician," the "Red Fox of Kinderhook," and the "American Talleyrand."

Van Buren had been a widower for eighteen years when he moved into the White House in 1837 with his four sons. Shortly afterward, his oldest son, Major Abraham Van Buren, a West Point graduate, married Angelica Singleton (above), a southern belle who was probably the most beautiful hostess the White House has ever known. Notwithstanding her graciousness, Angelica was criticized by many Washington dowagers, particularly after her return from her European honeymoon, for attempting to establish court airs and customs. It was her habit to wear three large ostrich plumes in her hair and receive her guests seated in an armchair on a raised platform. She was, incidentally, the first White House hostess to introduce the hoop skirt. Her elegant father-in-law meanwhile rolled around Washington in a magnificent olive-green coach with silver-mounted harness and liveried footmen.

In Washington City.

WHEN VAN BUREN WAS PRESIDENT: The city of Washington (left) had a population of about forty thousand. Pigs and chickens roamed the streets at will; slaves were sold openly; the terrain was swampy, malaria-ridden and crisscrossed by cowpaths and open sewers. Charles Dickens took a horrified look and wrote that the city's spacious avenues began in nothing and led nowhere, "streets miles long that only want houses, roads and inhabitants; public buildings that need but a public to complete."

"The Long Bill" is the title of the picture below which shows a customer in a typical country store of 1840 checking his account against the clerk's ledger, and perhaps symbolizes the hard times following the depression of 1837.

The rise of the factory system, a product of the Industrial Revolution, took place in America in the early part of the last century and by the time Van Buren was president innumerable mill towns had come into being, particularly in New England where water power was available. Above is a picture of a cotton factory village at Glastonbury, Connecticut, in the 1830s.

A HARD ROAD TO HOE!

The above 1840 campaign cartoon showing Van Buren, with his Subtreasury Bill on his back, being led to the White House by Jackson for a second term (it didn't come out that way) may have given rise to the expression "O.K." Partisans of the President formed an Old Kinderhook Club in 1840 and their rallying cry was "O.K." Thus, what was O.K. was good.

Van Buren's Subtreasury Bill, passed by Congress in June, 1840, was an effort to establish a system whereby the government would care for its own money in subtreasuries in the larger cities. It was repealed less than a year later, shortly after Van Buren left the White House. This cartoon (right) shows him leaving with the bill under his arm as Harrison, the new President, peers through the window and says, "Show the gentleman out. . . ." Actually, Van Buren personally welcomed Harrison to the White House and entertained him with great courtesy. He was the first president to welcome a successor from the opposite party.

A TIPPECANOE PROCESSION.

WILLIAM HENRY HARRISON
1773–1841
President 1841

"Keep the ball rolling" is another American expression that had its origin in 1840, when a group of Harrison supporters rolled a large paper ball (above) from Kentucky to Baltimore where the National Convention of Whig Young Men was held. "Keep the ball rolling on to Washington," was the cry.

Harrison was chosen by the Whigs to oppose Van Buren over men of greater ability in the party, mainly because there was nothing wrong with him. He had a good military record. He won a reputation as a daring Indian fighter under "Mad Anthony" Wayne in the Ohio forests in the 1790s. When he was governor of the Indiana Territory he led a force of nine hundred troops to victory at Tippecanoe (1811) and defeated the Shawnee Chief, Tecumseh, at the Battle of the Thames (1813), to become a national hero. He was the son of Benjamin Harrison, signer of the Declaration. Tall, slim and erect, he made an impressive figure

in the saddle. He did not drink or gamble and refused to be drawn into duels at a time when such practices were considered manly and the cause of much boasting. He was completely honest, happily married to a woman who bore him ten children, and was a representative of the new great West. He was a sure vote-getter, but best of all, perhaps, was the fact that he had not recently been active in politics and had no views upon current issues.

Harrison had run against Van Buren in 1836 and had made a poor showing. But now, after four years of Democratic rule, distasteful to many because of the 1837 depression and the too elegant habits of Van Buren, the stage was set for a change. Thurlow Weed, leader of the Whigs, maneuvered Harrison into the nomination just as he had done four years before. For his running mate, John Tyler of Virginia was chosen. The Whigs had no platform and avoided all issues. To hide their lack of principle they staged a theatrical campaign that bordered on hysteria. "Tippecanoe and Tyler Too" was the Whig slogan.

When it was sneeringly said by a Democratic writer that Harrison lived in a log cabin and had better remain there, the Whigs adopted the log cabin and hard cider as their emblem to show that their man was a plain country boy in contrast to the fancy, wine-drinking Van Buren. Although Harrison did not live in a log cabin (his house at North Bend, Ohio, had twenty-two rooms and was covered with clapboards) and was not born in one, and didn't drink cider, the emblem swept the country. The Log Cabin Campaign was a national frolic. In jubilant parades throughout the country, people carried log cabins and casks of hard cider.

At sixty-eight, Harrison was the

oldest president to be inaugurated and the first to die in office. His inaugural address (above), which incidentally was written by Daniel Webster, was the first to reach the country by railroad. People in Philadelphia were amazed when they were able to read the speech in the newspapers the very day it was delivered in Washington. Standing bareheaded without an overcoat in a raw wind, old Tippecanoe was inaugurated ninth president on March 4, 1841. Back home in North Bend his wife, Anna Symmes Harrison, was reluctantly getting ready to go to Washington. "I wish my husband's friends had left him happy and contented where he was," she said. By the end of the month Harrison fell ill with what was then called "bilious pleurisy" (probably pneumonia) and died on April 4, one month to a day after taking

the oath of office. His wife got the news just as she was about to depart. Harrison was the last president born a British subject.

JOHN TYLER 1790–1862
President 1841–1845

John Tyler was the first vice-president to reach the White House through the death of a president. When he got the news he was on his knees shooting marbles with his children in Williamsburg, Virginia. He didn't even know that Harrison had been sick when the chief clerk from the office of Secretary of State galloped into his yard with the message that he was president.

"Honest John" Tyler, a tall, thin man with a high-bridged nose and blue eyes, was kindly and well-mannered, but of less than mediocre

ability. He served without distinction as governor of Virginia and United States senator, and had it not been for Harrison's death his name would be buried in oblivion. Originally a Democrat, he was read out of the party for refusing to follow Jacksonian leadership and became a Whig —also became "Turnacoat Tyler" to his enemies. As a Whig he was put on the ticket with Harrison to draw southern votes, but since he sided with the Democrats more than half the time, the Whigs didn't like him either. Not many people did. Once after vetoing a banking bill his own party had endorsed, a mob of angry Whigs assembled outside the White House, hissed and abused him and burned him in effigy. Troubles thickened over his head. To show their bitter contempt, all of his Cabinet resigned with the exception of Daniel Webster, who remained only because of a treaty with England he was working on.

His first wife (above, left), Letitia Christian Tyler, the mother of seven of his fourteen children, was an invalid and died in September, 1842. Tyler did not endear himself to the country when two years later at the age of fifty-four he married twenty-four-year-old Julia Gardiner (above, right) whose father had been his friend. (This portrait of Julia was painted when she was twenty-eight. Later it was hung in the White House at the request of President Johnson —the first portrait of a president's wife to be so honored.)

On the credit side of Tyler's administration was the settlement of a boundary dispute with Canada and the suppression of the Seminole Indians. Both the Whigs and Democrats tossed him aside when his term was up and he retired to his Virginia home. He died in 1862 as a member of the Confederate Congress, in revolt against the United States.

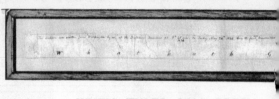

The American Indian worked crude copper mines (above) in the mineral-rich Lake Superior region long before the white man arrived. In 1844 a party of government surveyors accidently came across deposits of iron ore in the Lake Superior hills, which led to the discovery of the Mesabi range, the greatest iron-mining region in the world.

WHEN TYLER WAS PRESIDENT: Samuel F. B. Morse sent the first telegraphic message, "What hath God wrought?" from Washington to Baltimore on May 24, 1844. The strip of paper (above) on which the original message was recorded is now in the Library of Congress. One of America's greatest men, Morse invented the telegraph and the Morse code, was the most accomplished portrait painter of his day, the founder of the National Academy of Design, and (with John W. Draper) introduced the daguerreotype to this country.

This cartoon (left) appeared in the 1840s in answer to the followers of William Miller who predicted that the world would be destroyed by fire on April 23, 1843. The man in the fireproof safe, stocked with a supply of food and liquor, thumbs his nose at the world just before closing the door. Miller's prediction was taken seriously by thousands of converts throughout New England and up-state New York, who sold their property, donned white-robed ascension gowns and gathered on hilltops the morning of the great day. When nothing happened Miller said that he'd miscalculated the date, and named another. Again the Millerites, as they were called, went through the same thing. That was the end of the movement.

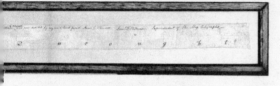

P. T. Barnum (right), the Prince of Humbugs, began his career in 1842 when he opened his "American Museum" of curios in New York City. Depicted here as a humbug, or fraud (the origin of the word is lost), Barnum was an extravagant advertiser and promoter. He presented Tom Thumb and Jenny Lind, and merged his circus with J. A. Bailey to form the famous Barnum and Bailey Circus, the "Greatest Show On Earth."

Daniel in the Lion's Den.

"THE FISH QUESTION WILL BE SETTLED, AS THE BULWER TREATY WAS, WITH THE BRITISH MINISTER OVER A BOTTLE OF BRANDY."—*Democratic Review.*

When Daniel Webster (left) was preparing a treaty with Great Britain to fix the Maine-Canadian boundary, he said that he would settle the matter with the British minister "over a bottle of brandy." The Democrats' response was this cartoon, a jibe at Webster's weakness for the bottle.

The steamboat and flatboat (right) flourished side by side on the Mississippi in the 1840s, floating more tonnage than all the rest of the country inland and ocean-going.

JAMES K. POLK 1795–1849
President 1845–1849

"Who is Polk?" the Whigs asked in derision when newspapers announced the name of the Democratic nomi- nee in 1844. "Who is Polk?" was soon taken up as their battle cry from one end of the nation to the other. A fitting answer was given some years later by Carl R. Fish, an American historian, who said: "He

was the least conspicuous man who had ever been nominated for President."

Short, slightly built and gray-eyed, the inconspicuous Polk was the first dark horse to become president. The Democratic convention at Baltimore quickly developed into a contest between Van Buren, seeking vindication for his defeat in 1840, and Lewis Cass of Michigan, who was preferred by western and southern delegates. Nobody thought of Polk. On the first ballot Van Buren polled 146 votes, a clear majority, but 30 votes short of the necessary two thirds. Cass got 83 votes. The two candidates were still leading the field on the seventh ballot and, as it has often happened since then, after some behind-the-scenes maneuvering, a compromise candidate was brought forth to break the deadlock. Polk's name first appeared on the eighth ballot (44 votes) and on the next he was the only contestant left in the field.

Well, who was Polk? He was a North Carolinian by birth, forty-nine years old, a graduate of the University of North Carolina (at the head of his class), a lawyer and member of Congress representing Tennessee for fourteen years (1825–1839), during which time he did not miss a sitting except for one day when he was confined to his bed by illness. A hard worker, respectable, and a staunch supporter of Andrew Jackson, people were already calling him "Young Hickory." It was Jackson who persuaded him to leave Congress where he served as Speaker of the House to run for governor of Tennessee. Polk was loath to leave, but being a good party man did as he was bade and won the governorship. In two later attempts he was twice defeated. That was Polk's record when the nomination was handed to him.

He was married to Sarah Childress Polk (above), who was a graduate of the Moravian Institute of Salem, North Carolina. Well-read and cultured, she was described by an English tourist as being "a very handsome woman. Her hair is very black and her dark eyes and complexion

remind one of the Spanish donnas."

A cold, hard rain fell on Washington's unpaved streets the day Polk was inaugurated (March 4, 1845). Splendid uniforms and plumed hats wilted in the downpour. The people in the plaza could scarcely see the President. He spoke, said John Quincy Adams, "to a large assemblage of umbrellas."

"This is the House That Polk Built" was the title of the above cartoon which appeared in the humorous publication *Yankee Doodle* in 1846. The frail house of cards beneath which the President sits like a broody hen (a reference to the plots he was hatching) was in danger of collapse, according to his critics. The Mexican War, the acquisition of California, the Oregon boundary settlement with England, the tariff, and Polk's bid for fame form the materials of the weak structure.

A more sympathetic view of Polk's Mexican War (the most important event of his administration) is shown in the cartoon above, right. Here Brother Jonathan (the forerunner of Uncle Sam as a symbol of America) has taken a good chunk out of the Mexican pie following the capture of Monterey. Hovering over the dish are France and England, both wishing some of the pie but "fearful of disturbing Jonathan at his meal." The tethered dog is General Santa Anna, who had seized the Alamo in 1836 and is now, ten years later, dictator and military leader of Mexico.

The two cartoons illustrate the difference of opinion of the people of the United States, who were split down the middle on the two paramount issues as Polk took office—the Oregon boundary dispute and the annexation of Texas which, as everyone knew, would mean war with Mexico.

The American claim to the Oregon region, then our only foothold on the Pacific, ran clear to Alaska; the British claim went down as far as Portland. One faction demanded war unless England yielded everything up to the parallel of latitude expressed in the phrase "fifty-four forty or fight!" The other faction shared Senator McDuffie's opinion of Oregon when he said that he "would not give a pinch of snuff for the whole territory." In a compromise treaty the forty-ninth parallel became the permanent dividing line.

As for the Mexican War, Polk was both vilified as an imperialist and hailed as a patriot. The expansionists demanded that we take all of Mexico; others, as expressed in a House resolution, branded the war as "unnecessarily and unconstitutionally begun by the President." The resolution was passed by a margin of four votes. Among those voting "aye" was a young congressman from Illinois named Abraham Lincoln.

CALIFORNIA REPUBLIC

WHEN POLK WAS PRESIDENT: The Halls of Montezuma were invaded when General Winfield Scott (above) took possession of Mexico City on September 14, 1847. The peace treaty provided for our acquisition of more than 500,000 square miles of territory in California and the Southwest, the recognition of our prior annexation of Texas and the establishment of the Rio Grande River as the boundary. For this Mexico got fifteen million dollars. Our casualties were 1,733 battle deaths, 8,034 wounded.

The above "Bear Flag" flew over the short-lived California Republic from June, 1846, until the following January.

A popular stage character in the 1840s was Mose the Fire-boy (below) as played by Francis S. Chanfrau. A Bowery tough attired in plug hat, red shirt and turned-up trousers, the impudent Mose represented the comic element of the New York underworld.

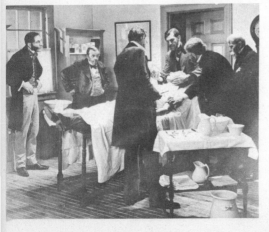

The first demonstration of the administration of ether (left) took place in the Massachusetts General Hospital, Boston, on October 16, 1846, when Dr. John C. Warren removed a tumor from the jaw of his patient, Gilbert Allen.

The above picture from *Scott's Fashions For Summer* shows what smartly dressed Americans wore in 1847. What they did not wear (except for a few suffragettes) was the costume (left) introduced by Amelia Bloomer of Seneca Falls, New York, in protest against the cumbersome hoop skirt.

The discovery of gold in California in 1848 resulted in the greatest mass migration in American history. In two years some 100,000 gold seekers stampeded to California, traveling cross-country, via Panama or around the Horn by ship.

The first baseball game of record was played on June 19, 1846, on the Elysian Fields, a summer resort in Hoboken, New Jersey, between two amateur Manhattan teams—the Knickerbockers and the New Yorks. The still-existing scorebook records that the New Yorks won the contest, 24 to 1.

GENERAL ZACHARIAH TAYLOR, (OLD ROUGH AND READY
As he appeared at the battle of Palo Alto: from a sketch by a lieutenant of Artillery

ZACHARY TAYLOR 1784–1850
President 1849–1850

Zachary Taylor was a hearty, to-bacco-chewing old Regular Army man who had little schooling, no knowledge of law, government or politics, and had never cast a vote in his life when the Whigs in 1848 decided that he was to be their man for the Presidency. "Old Rough and Ready," as his adoring troops called him, looked like anything but presidential timber. Short, dumpy and thick-necked, he had a head big enough to rest on the body of a

giant. His legs were so short that his orderly had to help him into the saddle whenever he mounted his favorite war horse, "Old Whitey." He had a big nose, puckering full lips and a permanent scowl. He was the most unmilitary-looking officer in the army and the higher he rose in rank the more careless he became in dress. His soldiers gave him his nickname because he rode before them wearing an old battered straw hat and a long linen duster, looking rough and ready. Once, a newly appointed lieutenant just out of West Point addressed him as "Say, old codger," thinking that the General was a camp follower. Later, when the young man discovered his mistake and apologized profusely, Taylor smiled and said, "Never judge a stranger by his clothes." Old Rough and Ready was a kindly man despite his crude manners and shabby appearance.

Five presidents before Taylor had seen war service, but only as citizen soldiers. He was the first Regular Army man to become president. After a short service as an enlisted man in the Kentucky militia he was given a first lieutenant's commission by President Jefferson in 1808, when he was twenty-four. For the next forty years he remained in the army. He advanced rapidly, winning merit for gallantry as an Indian fighter in the Northwest and in Florida, and again in the Black Hawk War. When Polk sent him to Mexico he won battle after battle, culminating with the overthrow of Santa Anna at Buena Vista.

As the hero of the Mexican War, a southerner and slaveholder, his popularity in the South seemed certain to the Whigs, while his military record would get votes in the North. They nominated him without knowing where he stood on any issue.

AN AVAILABLE CANDIDATE.
THE ONE QUALIFICATION FOR A WHIG PRESIDENT.

The anti-Taylor cartoons on this page show the Whig candidate (above) as a murderer perched on the skulls of his victims, and (below) refusing to tell his supporters where he stood on any issue. The slavery issue, whether it should be extended in the new territories or abolished altogether, was the most important one and the Whigs tried to evade it. In the election the Democratic vote was split between Cass, the regular candidate, and Van Buren, running on the Free-Soil (antislavery) ticket. The split enabled Taylor to win a plurality of the popular votes and 163 out of 290 electoral votes.

In his brief sixteen-month regime in the White House, Taylor took a surprisingly firm stand against southerners who threatened to secede, and said that he'd lead the army in person and hang them as traitors. Taylor died in the White House on July 9, 1850, after an illness of five days. His wife, Margaret Smith Taylor, who never appeared at White House functions, and who supposedly smoked a corncob pipe in the privacy of her rooms, outlived him by two years.

QUESTIONING A CANDIDATE

90

The Presidency never came within the grasp of the three Titans who served their country in various capacities during the first half of the last century. They were Daniel Webster (right), the magnificent New England orator who stood for the preservation of the Union and a strong federal government; John C. Calhoun of South Carolina, the champion of states' rights and a staunch defender of slavery; and Henry Clay of Kentucky, the "Great Compromiser," who endeavored to avoid the inevitable Civil War by placating both North and South. Twice defeated for the Presidency, he said, "I would rather be right than President." Below, Clay addresses the Senate for the last time (February 5, 1850). Calhoun died in 1850 and was followed two years later by both Clay and Webster.

WHEN TAYLOR WAS PRESI-DENT: The Knickerbocker Line of Brooklyn hauled passengers on its famous "Stage Coach 76," drawn by ten white horses (above). These large omnibuses soon gave way to the horse-drawn streetcar, the first of which appeared in New York City as early as 1832.

A New York mob of Anglophobes got out of hand on May 10, 1849, in front of the Astor Place Opera House where the English actor, William Macready, was scheduled to perform that night (below). Remembering the ill treatment the American actor, Edwin Forrest, had received in England some time before, the mob stormed the doors of the Opera House and tried to get at the innocent Macready. The militia, sent to quell the riot, got a shower of paving stones and was forced to fire on the crowd. Many people were severely wounded, twenty-two were killed. Macready barely escaped with his life, fled to Boston and sailed home.

From the crest of San Francisco's Telegraph Hill (above) incoming ships could first be spotted as they entered the Golden Gate, and the news of their arrival was flashed to the town. On the slopes of Telegraph Hill a city of tents housed the first gold seekers. In the Bay in 1850 there were often as many as five hundred ships at anchor, most of which were abandoned and left to rot, as passengers and crew joined the mad rush to the gold fields.

America enjoyed a brief spell of glory in the transatlantic steamship service when Edward Knight Collins, a New Englander, put four luxurious liners in operation in 1850 that outdid in speed and comfort the best that England's Cunard Line could offer. The Collins Lines steamers were 282 feet long, of some 2,800 tons and cost three million dollars each. Collins first put into service the *Atlantic* (right), then followed it with the *Pacific, Arctic* and *Baltic*. They beat the rival Cunarders across the Atlantic regularly by from seven to eighteen hours, sometimes crossing

in less than ten days. A disastrous sinking of the *Arctic,* the disappearance of the *Pacific* without a trace, and the withdrawal of government subsidy finished the line in 1858.

A typical frontier scene of the times is this gathering of neighbors, depicted below, for a flax scutching bee (the separation of the flax from the fiber by beating), which was always followed by a large meal and general festivities.

The Fox sisters (above, left to right: Margaret, Kate and Mrs. Fish) excited the country in 1850 by giving the first demonstrations of spirit rappings. Years later they confessed that they made the sounds themselves, by cracking their joints.

MILLARD FILLMORE 1800–1874
President 1850–1853

When Millard Fillmore was vice-president during Old Rough and Ready's brief residence in the White House, people said that he looked more like a president than the President himself. And it was true—as far as looks go. In contrast to the squat, sloppily attired Taylor (he used to walk the streets of Washington in a tall silk hat perched on the back of his head and a black broadcloth suit purposely made too large for him), the Vice-President was over six feet tall, erect of carriage, impressively handsome and always faultlessly groomed. In further contrast, he did not use tobacco in any form and disdained liquor to such an extent that he would seek a "temperance hotel" to stop in when he was away from home. Nor did he succumb to the pitfalls of gambling, except on one occasion when he was fifteen and won a turkey raffle at a New Year's Day gathering. "No persuasion could induce me to raffle again," wrote Fillmore fifty-six years later. "That was the beginning and end of my gambling . . . and I have never since gambled to the value of one cent."

The suffocatingly respectable Fillmore did take a gamble, however (and lost), when he signed the Fugitive Slave Act shortly after he became president. The Act was part of the Compromise of 1850 as a concession to the South, which had yielded to the North in agreeing to admit California as a free state. Fillmore gambled that the Act would be acceptable to the North and that his political position would thus be strengthened. Instead, the law was abhorrent to all Yankees, for it permitted slave owners to invade the North, seize any Negro they said was a fugitive and without process of law drag him back into servitude. Many free Negroes who had been living in the North for years were virtually kidnaped. The open defiance of the law created serious friction and more than ever widened the rift between the North and South. It marked the end of Fillmore's political career.

Uninspiring as Fillmore was as president, credit is due him for his ability to overcome the handicaps of an impoverished home and to rise to high office. He was born of New England parents in a log cabin at Locke, Cayuga County, in the Finger Lakes region of New York, on January 7, 1800. At fifteen he was bound out by his parents to serve an apprenticeship to a wool carder (clothmaker) at an annual salary of fifty-five dollars. A bright lad, young Millard spent his spare moments when he was not working on the carding machine, in reading, as shown in the above two pictures.

While serving his apprenticeship he attended a one-room country school and straightway fell in love with the pretty red-headed schoolma'am, Abigail Powers. Abigail helped him with his learning to the extent that he was soon able to teach school himself and earn enough money to read law. The picture below shows the Buffalo schoolhouse where Millard taught in 1822. Four years later Abigail and Millard were married. By this time he had been admitted to the bar and his political career was under way: New York assemblyman, member of Congress, state controller of New York, and vice-president.

Abilgail Powers Fillmore (left) stirred Washington social circles by establishing the first White House library (there wasn't even a Bible in the place when she arrived), and by installing the first bathtub. A greater stir was created when the Fillmores appeared in a splendid wine-colored carriage (above) which had seats of blue silk and silver-mounted harness. Presented to Abigail by the ladies of New York State, it cost two thousand dollars, the horses one thousand each.

Below, the Fillmores are saluted as they enter New York Harbor aboard the *Erie* (May, 1851) on their way to Dunkirk, New York, to open the New York and Erie Railroad.

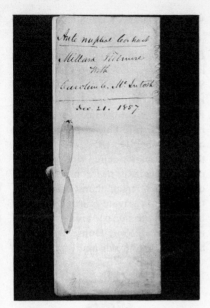

Fillmore suffered a blow to his pride in the convention of 1852 when his own party passed him over and nominated General Winfield Scott. Misfortune followed him about. A month after he left office Abigail was dead and a year later his only daughter died of cholera. In 1856 Fillmore ran for president as candidate of the American, or Know-Nothing party, and suffered a humiliating defeat, carrying only Maryland.

Two years later he married a wealthy widow, Mrs. Caroline C. McIntosh (above, right), but not until he had first drawn up a carefully worded marriage contract (above). This episode in Fillmore's life has no bearing on the Presidency, but is offered here as a commentary on the status of women in this country a hundred years ago when it was a man's world. By the terms of the contract he had complete control of her fortune "without being in any way accountable therefore." He re-ceived all profits and income from it and got her entire estate if he survived her. The one concession made was that should he die first, she would receive one third of his estate.

After his marriage Fillmore bought the largest mansion in Buffalo (below) and lived there with his wife until his death in 1874. She survived him by seven years. When Lincoln was assassinated, a mob, remembering Fillmore's southern leanings, surrounded the house, demanded that he drape it in black mourning cloth, and splashed ink on it.

WHEN FILLMORE WAS PRESIDENT: The most talked of woman in America was Jenny Lind, "The Swedish Nightingale" (left). Unknown in this country until P. T. Barnum brought her here for her first recital at Castle Garden, New York, on September 11, 1850, she captured the American public. Her pure soprano voice was heard in 137 cities during her triumphant tour. She traveled in a private railroad car (the first person to do so), visited the Fillmores at the White House, and made a fortune for herself and Barnum.

The accepted style in 1850 when mothers dressed their boys like this.

The yacht *America*, shown (left) leaving Boston Harbor in June, 1851, crossed the Atlantic and defeated a fleet of fourteen English yachts in a sixty-mile race around the Isle of Wight. The cup she brought back, known as "The America's Cup," has remained in this country's possession ever since.

Uncle Tom's Cabin (right) by Harriet Beecher Stowe, first published in book form on March 20, 1852, had a runaway sale of over 300,000 copies within a year in the United States, eventually a million in England. Ballads and plays followed in its wake. Its theme—the evils of slavery—exerted tremendous influence on American thought and probably did more to hasten the overthrow of slavery than anything else. The South replied with counterattacks against the northern factory system, but to no avail. Mrs. Stowe could still say, "The slaveowner can whip his slave to death." She got thousands of abusive letters from the South. In one was a black human ear.

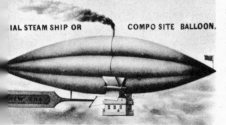

America was dreaming of the airship in 1850, or at least a stock promoter named Pennington was. He formed a company and sold shares to thousands of people in his aerial steamship (left). Needless to say, the great transoceanic ship was never constructed.

Abolitionists aiding the escape of slaves established the "Underground Railroad" with "stations" at regular intervals in northern towns and "conductors" to help them along. In 1850 an estimated twenty thousand slaves were brought north by this system. A notable escape was made by Henry Box Brown in 1850 (shown right emerging from a box), who got himself packed into a box three feet long, two and one-half feet deep and two feet wide, at Richmond, Virginia, and was shipped to Philadelphia and freedom.

FRANKLIN PIERCE 1804–1869
President 1853–1857

Franklin Pierce, shown above taking the oath of office on March 4, 1853, was a New Hampshire Democrat with strong southern sympathies who didn't like politics (he had resigned from the United States Senate and had turned down many political honors), didn't want to be president (he said that the office "would be utterly repugnant to my tastes and wishes") and was a dark-horse candidate unknown to the country. He made no speeches during his campaign. Pierce was the most unambitious man who ever ran for the Presidency. Yet he was elected by the most sweeping majority (254 electoral votes to his opponent's 42) since the second election of Monroe. The reason? First of all there was his opponent, the pompous, vainglorious General Winfield Scott, whose career in the now almost-forgotten Mexican War was his only qualification. Secondly, the Whig Party which

Scott represented faced both ways, as usual. In trying to please both North and South, the Whigs pleased no one. The party was disintegrating anyway. Its two greatest leaders, Clay and Webster, died in the midst of the 1852 campaign. And the country, having had three years of Whig rule under the unsatisfying leadership of Fillmore, was ready for a change. Almost anyone could have beaten Scott.

In picking Pierce, the Democrats put up a man who had a good military record (he served throughout the Mexican War), had an attractive personality and had no troublesome political record. As a candidate he supported the Compromise of 1850 —the chief issue of the day. Thus, the South liked him and the North tolerated him, mainly because of his Yankee background. He lost only four states.

Handsome Frank Pierce was a genial fellow who liked parties and gaiety and probably had more personal friends than any other presi-

dent. His lifelong friend was the novelist, Nathaniel Hawthorne, a classmate at Bowdoin, from which college he graduated in 1824. Another campus friend was Henry Wadsworth Longfellow. Of medium height, slim and erect, Pierce became a member of Congress and the United States Senate, and after the Mexican War returned to his Concord, New Hampshire, home to practice law. He was then forty-four and wanted only to remain where he was. He was still there five years later when he was suddenly lifted by the nape of the neck and set down in the White House.

In January, just before coming to Washington, the Pierces lost their third and last child, a boy of eleven, in a railroad wreck. They were with him at the time and saw him killed before their eyes. The shadow of the calamity hung over the White House. Except for an occasional assembly and a fortnightly presidential levee, there was little entertaining. The levee, once a regular White House function, was an informal gathering of people who came without formal invitation and dressed as they wished. The above picture shows Pierce receiving guests at a levee. His wife, Jane Appleton Pierce (left), was a sad little woman who rarely attended levees or any other social function. She hated Washington and most everything to do with the Presidency.

Pierce's regime was as unfortunate as his social life was drab. He alienated the North by his rigorous enforcement of the Fugitive Slave Act, and lost caste when abolitionists and proslavery immigrants poured into the newly opened Kansas territory and clashed, with much bloodshed.

Pierce was the only president who completed his term without making a single change in his Cabinet. Of the seven members, Secretary of War Jefferson Davis, soon to become president of the Confederacy, served with the greatest distinction. He enlarged the army and modernized its equipment, increased coastal and frontier defenses, reorganized the signal corps, and appointed subordinates on merit regardless of party.

WHEN PIERCE WAS PRESIDENT: Commodore Matthew Perry twice visited Japan with a squadron of American war vessels to seek trading rights with that country. Japan's door had long been closed to foreigners. President Fillmore initiated the open-door move, but Perry's negotiations and the subsequent signing of the United States-Japanese trade treaty (1854) took place during Pierce's administration. Left: officers and men of the United States squadron land at Simoda to meet the Imperial Japanese Commissioners.

In 1856 some thirty camels were brought to the United States for hauling freight across the desert country of Arizona and California (above).

"The Nantucket Sleigh Ride" (above), the most exciting and dangerous feature of whaling, when the mate, with the boat fast to a whale, approached for the kill. Whaling reached its zenith in the 1850s when Yankee ships sailed the seven seas.

After five years of labor and at the cost of more than eight hundred lives, the American-owned Panama Railroad was completed in 1855.

Above, the interior of the Meade Brothers Daguerreotype Gallery, New York, 1853.

This is a typical "Refreshment Salon" of the 1850s, catering to gentlemen only.

A DIRECTOR FORCED TO TRAVEL BY HIS OWN ROAD

Before the Civil War the annual death toll from railroad accidents was frightful—the result of cheaply and hastily constructed roads in an expanding country. One cure, as this cartoon (left) from the humorous publication *Lantern* indicates, was to force railroad directors to ride their own roads.

J. M. Studebaker went west to seek gold in 1853, but found that making wagons was more profitable. Right: the bearded Studebaker in his Hangtown, California, shop. Later he returned to Indiana and went into business with his brothers.

JAMES BUCHANAN 1791–1868
President 1857–1861

"Old Buck," our only bachelor president and the last to wear a stock, was the delight of political cartoonists who liked to feature the unruly tuft of hair crowning his head like a flame from a gas jet (above). Over six feet tall, blue-eyed and of distinguished appearance, he had the peculiarity of carrying his head slightly to one side "like a poll-parrot." This was because of poor vision, one eye being far-sighted, the other nearsighted. His political enemies during the 1856 campaign said that this was not the real reason for the tilted head. His neck, they said, had become permanently twisted in his attempt to hang himself some years before. The baseless lie was given wide credence.

Buchanan was another log cabin president, the son of an Irish immigrant who settled near Mercersburg, Pennsylvania. He attended Dickinson College in Carlisle, was admitted to the bar in 1812, and was such a brilliant young lawyer that at twenty-nine he was worth $300,000, all earned at law. About this time he became engaged to a gracious young woman named Anne Coleman, but she wrote him a letter of dismissal when gossips carried to her a false report of his supposed philanderings. Before he could set the matter straight Anne sickened and died. The tragedy stayed with him all his life. He was never interested in another woman.

For twelve years he was an unsuccessful candidate for the presidential nomination. Meanwhile, however, he served as congressman, United States senator, minister to Russia and Great Britain, and secretary of state. Although thrice defeated for the nomination, he had never been defeated in an election. This, perhaps, was one reason why the Democrats chose him over the futile Pierce who didn't care much about the nomination anyway. Moreover, Buchanan had been out of the country for three years (as minister to Great Britain) and had stayed out of trouble politically. Like Fillmore, and Pierce before him, he was a "doughface"—a word then used to describe a northern politician in sympathy with the South.

Mr. SHADBLOW, having voted for the successful candidate, resolves to be at the *inauguration*.

Having reached Washington, he goes to the Hotel and asks for "A Nice Room not too high up."

The "Gentlemanly Clerk" gives him his choice of the Roof or the Kitchen.—He prefers the latter.

Where he receives every attention from the former occupants of the Apartment.

In the morning he proceeds to the Barber's Shop for a "Wash and a Shave." He waits two hours for "his turn"—which does not come.

He returns to his room, and performs his ablutions as well as circumstances admit.

The glorious moment arrives. Mr. Shadblow witnesses the Inauguration—at a distance.

He thinks he will "drop in on Old Buck." But does not succeed.

He falls in with a "Member of the House," who introduces him to a "Senator."

Having parted with his Honorable Friends, he finds that he has lost his Pocket-Book.

What Washington was like at inauguration time nearly a century ago is shown in these sketches which appeared in *Harper's Monthly* magazine, April, 1857. The jammed hotels, uncomfortable quarters, the crowded city and the usual March weather that Mr. Shadblow had to endure are not too unlike the Washington scene today.

108

The White House as Buchanan knew it is shown in the above photograph, one of the first ever taken of the mansion. At that time the White House was gaslit, was heated by a furnace (installed by Pierce) and meals were cooked on a large iron stove which the Fillmores had put in. Buchanan had the interior renovated, and substituted American-made furniture for the work of French craftsmen. He did not live in the White House during the summer months because of the nearby malarial swamps, and predicted that it would soon be abandoned as a private residence and used only as an office.

In May, 1860, Buchanan received the first Japanese delegation ever to arrive in this country (right). Accompanied by an entourage of sixty people, the Japanese ministers brought expensive gifts to the President—embroidered saddles, swords, kimonos, writing cases, curtains and screens, a tea set valued at three thousand dollars and a cabinet that survived in the Green Room until Theodore Roosevelt had it removed forty-two years later.

THE LAYING OF THE CABLE—JOHN AND JONATHAN JOINING HANDS.

WHEN BUCHANAN WAS PRESIDENT: He received greetings from Queen Victoria upon the occasion of the opening of the first transatlantic cable (August, 1858), but, fearing that it was a hoax, delayed answering until her message was confirmed. The cable broke shortly afterward and was silent until it was repaired eight years later.

Edwin L. Drake erected the first oil well (below) at Titusville, Pennsylvania, in 1859, beginning the modern oil industry.

The Overland Mail service to the Pacific Coast was begun in 1858 (above). Coaches ran between Tipton, Missouri, and San Francisco.

Farnborough, England, was the scene of an international prize fight on April 17, 1860, when American champion John C. Heenan fought a forty-two-round draw with the British title-holder, Tom Sayers (above).

Left, John Brown, abolitionist fanatic, goes to his doom (December 2, 1859) following his unsuccessful raid at Harper's Ferry.

Traveling incognito as Baron Renfrew, the nineteen-year-old Prince of Wales (later Edward VII) visited this country in 1860 and laid a wreath on Washington's tomb at Mount Vernon (above) in company with the President.

Harriet Lane, Buchanan's niece, was a tall, auburn-haired beauty of twenty-five when she became mistress of the White House. Well trained in the social graces, intelligent and popular, Miss Harriet (she didn't marry until she was thirty-six) brought gaiety back into the White House, and made a perfect hostess for her ageing uncle.

OUT OF A SITUATION.

MRS. COLUMBIA.—WELL, BRIDGET, I GUESS WE SHA'N'T WANT YOUR SERVICES AFTER NEXT MARCH.
BIDDY BUCHANAN.—AN' SHURE THIN WILL YEZ BE AFTHER GIVING ME BACK ME CHARACKTHER?

The above cartoon, published in *Vanity Fair* magazine on April 7, 1860, correctly foretold what would happen to Buchanan at the end of his term. He would be dismissed by the American people and sent back to Wheatland, his Pennsylvania farm. Buchanan was sent back because he faced both ways on the growing crisis of slavery. He tried to appease the South by offering to make Kansas a slave state so that the number of free and slave states would be equal. He said that the southern states had no legal right to secede but, on the other hand, if they did the federal government had no legal right to put down the rebellion. While pondering this fine legalistic question which dis-

pleased both North and South, the Union fell to pieces and, as predicted, in March, 1861, the services of the tired, sixty-nine-year-old Buchanan were no longer wanted.

The first news to reach the Pacific Coast of Lincoln's election was carried across the plains by the Pony Express (below).

113

ABRAHAM LINCOLN 1809–1865
President 1861–1865

The country first heard the story of Lincoln's life a few months before his nomination, when at the request of a Republican friend he wrote a letter briefly sketching his career. An article based on the material was widely printed. But in the original letter (quoted here with some omissions) is Lincoln as he really saw himself:

"I was born February 12, 1809, in Hardin County, Kentucky. My parents were both born in Virginia, of undistinguished families—second families, perhaps I should say. My mother, who died in my tenth year, was of a family of the name of Hanks . . . My paternal grandfather, Abraham Lincoln, emigrated from Rockingham County, Virginia, to Kentucky about 1781 or 1782, where a year or two later he was killed by Indians, not in battle, but by stealth, when he was laboring to open a farm in the forest . . .

"My father, at the death of his father, was but six years of age, and he grew up literally without education. He removed from Kentucky to . . . Indiana in my tenth year . . . It was a wild region, with many bears and other wild animals still in the woods. There I grew up. There were some schools, so called, but no qualification was ever required of a teacher beyond 'readin', writin', and cipherin' ' to the rule of three . . . There was absolutely nothing to excite ambition for education. Of course, when I came of age I did not know much. Still, somehow, I could read, write, and cipher . . . but that was all. I have not been to school since."

Lincoln then summarized his career: general farm work until he was twenty-two; a clerk in a store at New Salem, Illinois; captain of volunteers in the Black Hawk War; member of the Illinois Legislature for eight years (during which time he studied law); member of Congress; law practice at Springfield, Illinois.

Without mentioning his wife or family, Lincoln closed his letter as follows: "If any personal description of me is thought desirable, it may be said I am, in height, six feet four inches, nearly; lean in flesh, weighing on an average of one hundred and eighty pounds; dark complexion, with coarse black hair and grey eyes. No other marks or brands recollected."

The one-room log cabin that Tom Lincoln moved into near Hodgenville, Kentucky, was little more than a shelter. It had a dirt floor, a window space, a fireplace of logs lined with clay and a bed made of slabs nailed to the wall. Here Abraham was born on February 12, 1809. Two years later Tom abandoned the worthless farm, tried another place at Knob Creek and again failed to make a permanent home. In 1816 he moved north to the Indiana wilderness where his wife, Nancy Hanks Lincoln, died of "milk-sickness" in the fall of 1818. Without the influence of a woman the family (Tom, his two children Abe and Sarah, and Dennis Hanks) sank almost into squalor for over a year. Then Tom took a second wife—Sarah Bush Johnston (left), a kind and gentle widow who brought her three children to the Lincoln cabin. Young Abe adored his stepmother and she in turn adored him and the other motherless children. When Lincoln as a man said, "God bless my mother; all that I am or ever hope to be, I owe to her," he was speaking of his stepmother.

These illustrations depicting scenes in Lincoln's early life show him, above: reading before the fireplace; below: his first flatboat trip, from Indiana to New Orleans when he was nineteen; right: delivering a letter as postmaster of New Salem, Illinois (1833–1836).

Lincoln's first photograph (1846), as a member of Congress, aged thirty-seven.

Mary Todd, a few years after her marriage to Lincoln in 1842.

In Springfield, Illinois, Lincoln lived in this house from 1844 until he moved to the White House. When he bought the house it had one and a half stories and contained a woodshed and a privy. The above photograph, taken in 1860, shows Lincoln in the yard with his two sons, Willie and Tad. At this time the house had been enlarged to two stories.

Lincoln was losing interest in politics when he was aroused by the passage of the Kansas-Nebraska Act in 1854, which meant that slavery could be extended into new territories. The sponsor of the bill was Stephen A. Douglas, the "Little Giant," once a suitor for Mary Todd's hand and now the Democratic senator from Illinois. As the Republican candidate for the United States Senate in 1858, Lincoln challenged Douglas to argue the great issue of the day in a series of debates across the state (left). "A house divided against itself cannot stand," said Lincoln as the debates began. "I believe this government cannot endure permanently half slave and half free . . . It will become all one thing, or all the other."

As a result of the debates, Lincoln rose from obscurity to become a figure of national importance, even though he lost the senatorial election to Douglas. "It is a slip and not a fall," he said of the defeat. His words proved true, for two years later he was nominated for president by the Republicans at Chicago. In a four-cornered race Lincoln fell short of a majority, but won the election because the hopelessly split Democrats divided their votes between Douglas and John C. Breckinridge, with a large number of votes going to John Bell of the new Constitutional Union party.

While Lincoln was on his way to Washington, it was discovered that an attempt on his life might be made as he passed through Baltimore. The planned itinerary was abandoned and he went straight to Washington, arriving there ahead of schedule at six o'clock on the morning of February 23, 1861, under guard (right).

Shortly before noon on March 4 the President-elect was driven in Buchanan's open carriage down Pennsylvania Avenue to the inauguration (below). High above him was the unfinished dome of the Capitol—symbolic of the unfinished Union.

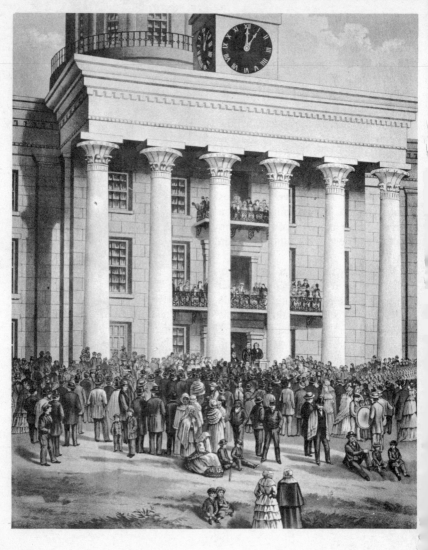

On February 18, just two weeks before Lincoln took the oath of office, Jefferson Davis was inaugurated president of the "Confederate States of America" at Montgomery, Alabama (above).

As the states seceded there was a clamor in the North to let the "wayward sisters depart in peace." Several measures were proposed in Congress for making a truce, or some kind of a compromise with the South. Even William H. Seward, Lincoln's Secretary of State, was against putting down the rebellion, believing that the South if let alone would soon return to the Union. But Lincoln stood firm, never wavering from his fixed purpose—the preservation of the Union. If it meant war, then war it would be even though he knew that the United States Army numbered less than fifteen thousand officers and men scattered over the nation. All eyes were turned toward him to see what he would do about Fort Sumter in Charleston Harbor where federal troops had been holding out against Confederate shore batteries. So far there had been no firing, but if Lincoln sent supplies the shooting would

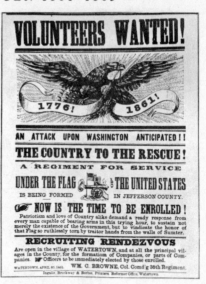

VOLUNTEERS WANTED!

1776! 1861!

AN ATTACK UPON WASHINGTON ANTICIPATED ! !

THE COUNTRY TO THE RESCUE !

A REGIMENT FOR SERVICE

UNDER THE FLAG OF THE UNITED STATES

IS BEING FORMED IN JEFFERSON COUNTY.

☞ NOW IS THE TIME TO BE ENROLLED !

Patriotism and love of Country alike demand a ready response from every man capable of bearing arms in this trying hour, to sustain not merely the existence of the Government, but to vindicate the honor of that Flag so ruthlessly torn by traitor hands from the walls of Sumter.

RECRUITING RENDEZVOUS

Are open in the village of WATERTOWN, and at all the principal villages in the County, for the formation of Companies, or parts of Companies. ☞ Officers to be immediately elected by those enrolled.

WATERTOWN, APRIL 20, 1861. WM. C. BROWNE, Col. Comd'g 35th Regiment.

Ingalls, Brockway & Beebe, Printers Reformer Office, Watertown.

begin. Knowing this, he notified the Governor of South Carolina on April 8 of his intention to supply the fort with provisions. Four days later the Confederates opened fire and the Civil War began.

At the outset of the war Lincoln's paramount object was to restore the Union, and not, as he said, "either to save or destroy slavery." By the middle of 1862, however, Confederate military triumphs and Lincoln's hands-off policy on slavery had dampened the enthusiasm of many northerners for the war. The Union cause needed bolstering, as Lincoln well knew. "We had about played our last card, and must change our tactics, or lose the game," he said. He decided on the Emancipation Proclamation as a necessary measure for the successful continuance of the war. Lincoln read a draft of the document to his Cabinet on July 22, 1862, and (according to the above inaccurate picture) to a stray pickaninny. Published to the world on the following New Year's Day, the Proclamation strengthened the Union cause in the North and in England. An unkind view of its effects is shown in this cartoon (left), from *Harper's Weekly,* January 17, 1863.

CUTTING HIS OLD ASSOCIATES.
Man of Color. "Ugh! Get out, I ain't one oh you no more. I'm a Man, I is!"

LINCOLN'S TWO DIFFICULTIES.

In England there was a sharp division of opinion on the American war. The British masses strongly opposed slavery and regarded the North as fighting for human liberty. The ruling class, however, looked upon the North as more or less of a rabble and favored the South. These cartoons from *Punch* reflect the opinion of the British upper classes. The one on the left shows Lincoln, in the guise of Uncle Sam, standing between a tax collector and a soldier. He says, "What? No Money! No Men!" When this cartoon appeared, the Union was far stronger than the Confederacy in both men and money, but *Punch* refused to believe it. An even blinder view is represented in the cartoon below, published in September, 1864. By that time Grant had won the West, and Lee had been turned back at Gettysburg. Mobile, New Orleans and Atlanta had fallen. The war was all but over. In a few weeks Lincoln would again triumph at the polls. Mrs. North did not fire her attorney.

MRS. NORTH AND HER ATTORNEY.

Mrs. North. "YOU SEE, MR. LINCOLN, WE HAVE FAILED UTTERLY IN OUR COURSE OF ACTION; I WANT PEACE, AND SO, IF YOU CANNOT EFFECT AN AMICABLE ARRANGEMENT, I MUST PUT THE CASE INTO OTHER HANDS."

WHEN LINCOLN WAS PRESI-
DENT: Many people forgot about
the Civil War in their frantic rush to
Oil Creek Valley, Pennsylvania
(above), to seek sudden wealth from
the new liquid gold. The drilling of
the first oil well at Titusville touched
off the stampede. In the remote lum-
bering region towns sprang up overnight, and towns became cities within
a week. As throngs poured in, farms
that had been valued at ten dollars a
square mile were sold at hundreds of
dollars a square inch. Nothing like it
had been seen since the California
Gold Rush of '49.

The Pony Express (above), with
relays of horsemen ten to fifteen
miles apart between St. Joseph, Missouri, and Sacramento, California,
averaged about two hundred miles
in twenty-four hours. It operated
from April, 1860, until October,
1861, when telegraph wires were installed.

The "Kerbstone Stockbrokers in
New York" (left) traded actively in
war securities and oil stocks during
the Civil War. Founded in 1849, the
Curb Exchange went indoors in 1921
and in 1953 changed its name to The
American Stock Exchange.

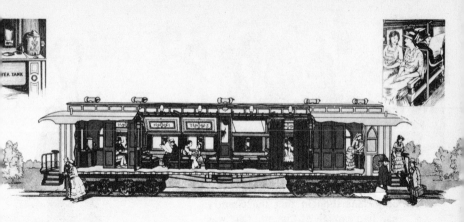

The first real **Pullman** sleeping car was the "Pioneer" (above), constructed in 1865. Much longer, higher and wider than its predecessors, which were rebuilt day coaches, the "Pioneer" was the first to have the folding upper berth. It was heated by a hot-air furnace, lighted with candles and had eight sections with two compartments at each end. The sixteen wheels tried at this period were later abandoned for twelve.

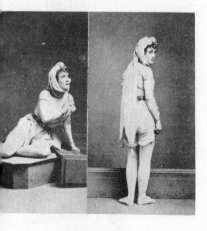

Two events in the entertainment world made New Yorkers forget the war. One was the appearance of Adah Isaacs Menken, "Enchantress of Men" (above), in the play *Mazeppa*. The other (right) was the marriage of Barnum's midgets, Tom Thumb and Lavinia Warren.

Early in 1864 many Republican politicians thought that the country had had enough of Lincoln. One was Thurlow Weed, a canny appraiser of popular opinion, who said that "the people are wild for peace" and that Lincoln's "re-election is an impossibility." Horace Greeley, editor of the New York *Tribune,* wrote: "Mr. Lincoln is already beaten. He cannot be elected. We must have another ticket to save us from utter overthrow." However, the Republicans, calling themselves the National Union Party, nominated Lincoln on the first ballot. To have done otherwise would have been an admission that his war policy was a failure. The Democratic candidate was General George B. McClellan, former leader of the Union forces, who had been fired by Lincoln. The President accepted the nomination without elation, saying that he supposed the convention had concluded "that it is not best to swap horses while crossing the river." "Don't swap horses" became the Unionist rallying cry. The election was an overwhelming victory for Lincoln who polled 212 electoral votes to McClellan's 21. (Above, soldiers of the Army of the Potomac cast their ballots.) In the soldier vote Lincoln scored heavily—116,887 votes against 33,748 for McClellan.

Long Abraham Lincoln a Little Longer

"Long Abraham a Little Longer" appeared in *Harper's Weekly* (above) after the election.

128

Reeling under Grant's blows south of Richmond, Lee knew that his weakened army could not hold out much longer, and on March 26 notified Jefferson Davis that the city must be abandoned. A few days later when the news of its surrender to General Weitzel reached Lincoln, he decided to visit the conquered city. On April 4 the President, with his twelve-year-old son Tad, Admiral Porter and an escort of twelve seamen armed with carbines, entered the Confederate Capital (below). They trudged two miles through the streets of the city, much of which had been fired by the retreating Rebels. All along the way worshipful Negroes hailed the President. To one who fell on his knees before him, Lincoln said, "Don't kneel to me. You must kneel to God only and thank Him for your freedom." When he arrived at the Execu-

GRANT TURNING LEE'S FLANK.

tive Mansion looking "pale, haggard, and utterly worn out," General Weitzel questioned him about the treatment of the conquered people. "If I were in your place, I'd let 'em up easy, let 'em up easy," Lincoln replied.

On the night of April 14, 1865, the President and his wife and their guests, Major Henry Rathbone and Clara Harris, sat in one of the four boxes in Ford's Theater, Washington, to watch a performance of the comedy, *Our American Cousin*. At about ten-fifteen during the third act John Wilkes Booth, a prominent actor, entered the box, fired his single-shot Derringer, and with his dagger stabbed Rathbone in the arm.

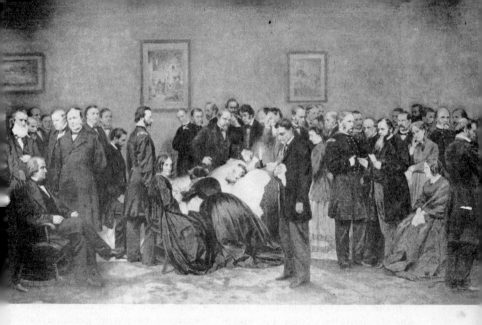

As Booth leaped from the balustrade to the stage, the spur on his right foot caught in a flag draping the box and he fell with such force that he broke a bone in his left leg. Brandishing his dagger as he limped across the stage, Booth shouted something that sounded like *"Sic semper tyrannis"* (ever thus to tyrants), and disappeared into the wings. A piercing scream came from the box. Immediately the theater became a scene of terror. Shouting, frenzied people rushed into the aisles and poured onto the stage. An army surgeon entered the box and upon examining the wound knew that it was fatal. Tenderly, the long lanky form of the President was carried across the street into a lodginghouse owned by William Peterson. In a small first-floor bedroom, Lincoln was placed upon a bed, diagonally, because of his great height. Throughout the night government officials and members of the family stood by, knowing that the end was near.

When it came, at seven twenty-two in the morning, Secretary Stanton said, "Now he belongs to the ages."

Booth had been recognized by many people at Ford's Theater. Soon his accomplices were known and the man hunt was on.

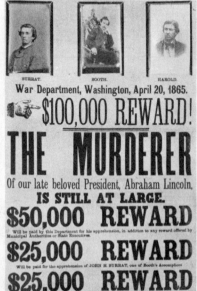

SURRAT.   BOOTH.   HAROLD.

War Department, Washington, April 20, 1865.

$100,000 REWARD!

THE MURDERER

Of our late beloved President, Abraham Lincoln,

IS STILL AT LARGE.

$50,000 REWARD

Will be paid by this Department for his apprehension, in addition to any reward offered by Municipal Authorities or State Executives.

$25,000 REWARD

Will be paid for the apprehension of JOHN H. SURRAT, one of Booth's Accomplices.

$25,000 REWARD

a fantastic plot to kidnap the President and deliver him to the Confederacy, which could then bargain to end the war on its own terms. Nothing came of the scheme, so Booth, after Lee's surrender, determined to avenge the South by killing Lincoln. From Ford's Theater, Booth fled on horseback out of Washington with one of his accomplices, a moron named David Herold. A few days later they rowed across the Potomac (left) into Virginia and continued south to the farm of Richard Garrett near Port Royal. Garrett thought that the men were returning Confederate soldiers. Here, on April 26, they were discovered by pursuing Union cavalrymen. Trapped in a burning tobacco barn, Herold surrendered, but Booth held out and was fatally shot through the neck by a soldier who fired without orders.

Booth was a show-off, ham actor who favored the South but spent most of the four war years in the North and never fought for the Confederacy. Toward the end of 1864 he collected a group of misfits in sympathy with the South and hatched

Seven of Booth's accomplices were quickly rounded up and given a military trial before uniformed judges selected by the War Department. Of the seven tried, four were condemned to death, the others receiving life imprisonment. The execution took place in a Washington jailyard on July 7, 1865, as shown in the photograph and the drawing on this page. The condemned (from left to right) were: Mrs. Mary Surratt, who kept the boardinghouse where Booth's men met; Lewis Powell, alias Payne, who tried to kill Secretary of State Seward as part of Booth's wholesale assassination plot; David Herold, who helped Booth escape; and George Atzerodt, a German-born Confederate spy who was assigned to kill Vice-President Johnson, but lost his nerve.

Numerous appeals had been sent to President Johnson in the hope that Mrs. Surratt might be saved, for there was some question of her guilt. But the President was adamant. "She kept the nest where the egg was hatched," he replied.

EXECUTION OF THE CONSPIRATORS.

A black-draped funeral car (below) bore Lincoln's body on the last journey from Washington to Springfield. For 1,700 miles the car moved across the country, stopping along the way at many cities where the body was taken from the car to lie in state. (Above, the funeral cortege at Columbus, Ohio.) The journey began at Washington on April 21 and ended in Springfield, May 3.

Lincoln's remains were first interred in a public receiving vault in Oak Ridge Cemetery, Springfield (above), later removed to a temporary vault until the completion of the final resting place which was dedicated in 1874. Here buried with him are his wife and three sons, Eddie, Willie and Tad. Robert, the first-born son, was the last surviving member of the family. He lived until 1926 when he died in his eighty-third year after a notable career: secretary of war, minister to England and president of the Pullman Company. Mary Todd Lincoln died in 1882, aged sixty-four. She was a storm center during her White House reign. Erratic and unpredictable, she was at once warmhearted and quarrelsome —"Quick to speak, quick to repent." She lavished money on clothes and went deeply into debt. Two years after she left Washington and put her finery on public sale, the country was astounded at the inventoried values: a bolt of lace at four thousand dollars; a shawl at two thousand, and so on. A loyal and devoted wife through the lean years of her husband's career, she was a failure in the White House. In 1875 she was adjudged insane.

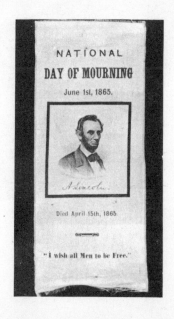

NATIONAL
DAY OF MOURNING
June 1st, 1865.

A. Lincoln

Died April 15th, 1865.

"I wish all Men to be Free."

ANDREW JOHNSON 1808–1875
President 1865–1869

Andrew Johnson, the only president who never spent a single day in a schoolroom, was a "poor white" born of lowly parentage in a shack that still stands at Raleigh, North Carolina. His father, a janitor, died when Andy was three and a few years later the lad and his older brother were bound out to a tailor, to be fed and clothed for their work until they became twenty-one. After two years of bondage both boys ran away, worked for a while as journeymen tailors in South Carolina, and upon their return to Raleigh found that a reward of ten dollars had been posted for their capture. Consequently, they went to Eastern Tennessee where Andy opened a tailor shop in Greenville (above). In this mountain town he married Eliza McCardle who taught him to read and write. An apt pupil with a flair for oratory, he soon got into politics and battled his way upward to the United States Senate. Although he was a Southern Democrat and a slaveowner, Johnson alone among the twenty-two southern senators had the courage to stand up against an overwhelming sentiment in his own state and fight secession. At Lincoln's request he left the Senate to take the job of military governor of Tennessee. While he was serving in that post he was nominated vice-president.

Johnson was solidly built and stood five feet nine inches. He had an Indian-like swarthiness—black hair, deep-set dark eyes and a mouth with lines of grim determination. The hard expression may well have been caused by the many bitter battles he fought and the abuse heaped upon him. No president was ever so vilified. To the South he was "white trash" and a traitor. To the fire-eaters of the North, who wanted the Rebels punished more severely, he was a turncoat. To both he was a drunkard. This accusation was the result of his condition at the time of his inauguration as vice-president. A short time before the ceremonies Johnson, who had been ill, felt faint and asked for a stimulant. He drank three glasses of brandy. When he entered the Senate Chamber he was sober but the hot, crowded room had its effect and he made a rambling, incoherent speech. Johnson was always a moderate drinker, but this one unfortunate happening caused him to be branded as a drunkard.

The President's wife (above) was a quiet, sweet-dispositioned woman who was so weakened by tuberculosis that she made only one public appearance during her almost four years' residence in the White House. The First Lady duties were assumed by her married daughter, Martha Johnson Patterson.

When Johnson first came to the Presidency he insisted upon personal punishment of the Rebel leaders and economic punishment of the whole South. But he soon softened his tune and issued a Proclamation of Amnesty, which was a general pardon to all who were in the Rebellion, provided that they took an oath of loyalty to the Union. Not included were the leaders of the Confederacy and persons worth over twenty thousand dollars. In less than nine months after the Proclamation some fourteen thousand southerners received pardons from the President. The picture below shows Johnson receiving a group of Rebels in the White House.

The fall of the Confederacy left the South bankrupt with four million free Negroes on its hands, only one tenth of whom could read or write. To alleviate the general chaos, George Peabody, a New Englander by birth and a wealthy international banker, created a two-million-dollar fund (later increased to three and one-half million) for the advancement of education in the South. In the above idealistic conception, Peabody surveys the harmonious scene from a flag-draped chariot as Union generals beat their swords into plowshares and transform a cannon into a millrace. Negroes emerge from the wilderness of ignorance, children romp joyfully and northern workers arrive to aid their southern brethren. That it was not so harmonious is in-

dicated in this cartoon (below) which shows Johnson protesting while General Sheridan administers the physic of reconstruction to the South.

THE RECONSTRUCTION DOSE.

NAUGHTY ANDY—"*Don't take that physic, Sis, it's nasty—kick his shins.*"

MRS. COLUMBIA—"*My dear Andy, don't be a bad boy, don't interfere—Dr. Congress knows what's best for Sissy.*"

In the fall of 1866 Johnson made a speaking tour of the East and Middle West, trying to rally opinion against the Republican radicals who were demanding severe punishment of the South. With him went General Grant, Admiral Farragut and Secretary Seward. No president ever suffered such humiliation as Johnson did on this tour. In almost every city mobs shouted him down: "Shut up, Johnson, we don't want to hear from you!" Nowhere was he protected against the insults. The cheers were all for Grant (below). Johnson's mission—the restoration of the South through conciliation—was a failure.

The cartoons on this page are from humorist Petroleum V. Nasby's account of the tour, *Andy's Trip to the West*. Scurrilously unfair, Nasby sees Johnson (below) as a goose—a reference to a tailor's goose, or flatiron. The bottom picture is captioned: "He is supported by Secretary Seward." (The accusation by Johnson's enemies that he appeared drunk on the tour is without foundation.) In the right column, from top to bottom, the captions read: "He hears from Maine." "He hears from Pennsylvania, Indiana and Ohio." "He hears from New York." Here Nasby may have been right, for the tour got progressively worse.

More humiliation was Johnson's lot when a House committee prepared impeachment charges against him for "high crimes and misdemeanors." Above, a ticket to the trial. Below, Sergeant-at-arms George T. Brown serves the President at the White House the summons to appear before the High Court of Impeachment.

The impeachment stemmed from the difficulties between Johnson and his Secretary of War, Edwin M. Stanton, a radical Republican who was openly insubordinate to the President. Fearing that Stanton might be removed, the Radicals passed an act forbidding the President to fire his own Cabinet members. This insult enraged Johnson and he promptly dismissed Stanton, but the Secretary refused to leave his office. Now the Radicals had grounds to bring charges against the President. His defense was that such a law was unconstitutional. The trial was held by the whole Senate (March 13–May 26, 1868) and resulted in a vote of 35 for conviction, 19 against, just one vote short of the necessary two thirds (or 36) for conviction. Thus, by one vote Johnson was acquitted. A few months later his term ended and he returned to Tennessee. But he came back to Washington in 1875 when the people of his state returned him to the United States Senate. Personal vindication was his at last.

Jeff Davis (above) hotfooted it out of Richmond the day before Lincoln entered it, fled south with his Cabinet and was captured by Union soldiers at Irwinville, Georgia, on May 10, 1865. Andrew Johnson, who once said that he'd hang the Rebel President to a tree, changed his mind and even promised that he wouldn't have him turned over to a military commission. Davis was imprisoned in Fortress Monroe where he spent some time in irons. Two years later he was released on bail furnished by Horace Greeley and Cornelius Vanderbilt, pending a future trial. It was never called. He spent the last years of his life in retirement at Biloxi, Mississippi. He died in 1889.

"Seward's Icebox" was the name given to Alaska when the territory was purchased from Russia in 1867

for $7,200,000. In the above cartoon Secretary of State Seward and the President haul off the worthless block of ice. The unpopular Johnson was virtually ignored by the press when he died in 1875, as evidenced by this brief *Harper's Weekly* obituary (below).

ULYSSES S. GRANT 1822–1885
President 1869–1877

Ulysses S. Grant was a shy, stumpy little man (five feet, eight inches) who hated war and hated politics, yet he was the most successful mili-

tary leader of the Civil War and was twice elected to the Presidency. The man who was called "Grant the Butcher" during the war because of the way he drove his troops to wholesale slaughter, was horrified of game hunting and could never shoot an

animal or bird. Although he was schooled in war and the rough life of military outposts where profanity was freely used, he never swore—not even a mild "damn"—and off-color stories revolted him. His physical modesty was extreme. During the Civil War he would carefully close the flaps of his tent before taking a bath so that no one could see him, unlike his fellow officers who had their orderlies pour pails of water over them in the open. Years later he said that no one had seen him naked since he was a small boy. Inexplicable in many ways was Grant. Lacking drive or decision in civilian life, he was a failure in everything he did. But in war he was a lion—determined and relentless, and an efficient organizer. "Unconditional Surrender" Grant was the name he earned when he demanded those terms of Confederate General Buckner at Fort Donelson. Yet no one was more magnanimous to a beaten foe. At heart Grant was a pacifist all his life. "I never liked service in the army," he said some years after the war was over. "I did not wish to go to West Point . . . I never went into a battle willingly or with enthusiasm, and I never want to command another army." He never owned a military book of any kind—as the citizens of Boston found out to their amazement when they presented him with a library of five thousand volumes.

Upon his graduation from West Point, Grant was sent to Jefferson Barracks, St. Louis, where he met Julia Dent (above), the daughter of a slave-owning farmer. Within a year the couple became engaged, but did not marry until Grant returned from the Mexican War four years later. Julia Dent Grant was by no means a beauty. Her features were plain and she had a cast in one eye which caused her to squint. But she was amiable, tactful and devoted to her husband. As First Lady she considered an operation to correct the eye defect, but the President persuaded her not to have it done. He liked her, he said, with her eyes crossed and would not have her different.

When the seventeen-year-old lad (born Hiram Ulysses Grant but changed to Ulysses Hiram so that his initials wouldn't be "H.U.G.") arrived at West Point in 1839 he found that he was registered as Ulysses Simpson Grant, due to an error made by the congressman who appointed him. Grant never bothered to change the name back. As a cadet he was below average in studies and con-duct. In marks he stood 21 in a graduating class of 39, and in con-duct 156 among 223 cadets in the entire corps. A large number of his demerits came from sloppiness of dress and for being late at roll calls. He was, however, the best horseman in the corps. The above picture, drawn from a daguerreotype, shows him as a young lieutenant shortly after his graduation.

Grant served as regimental quartermaster throughout the Mexican War and saw action in several battles. Among his comrades-in-arms were Robert E. Lee and Jefferson Davis, who were to oppose him a few years later in a greater struggle. After the war he was assigned to dreary frontier posts on the Pacific Coast. Lonely and homesick, and hating the army, Grant took to drinking and consumed more than his share—so much more that his resignation from the army was requested. From then (1854) until the Civil War broke out he was an abject failure—an unsuccessful farmer living in a log cabin (below) on land owned by his father-in-law, a peddler of firewood in St. Louis (right), a real estate agent, and a clerk under his younger brothers in the family leather store at Galena, Illinois. He was then at the low point of his career, a forlorn figure still seeking solace in the bottle. The thirty-nine-year-old failure began his climb to fame in 1861 when he

1859—ST. LOUIS.

offered to drill a company of Galena volunteers. Three years after leaving Galena he was in command of all the United States armies. Four years later he was elected president. No American ever rose from such depths to such heights in so short a time.

Grant, the bulldog, rolled up a string of victories in the West: Fort Henry, Fort Donelson, and Shiloh (above), where he led a charge which ended in a full Confederate retreat. Even so, there was criticism of him in the press. It was charged that

no respect was felt for him by his men, that he sometimes disappeared after an engagement (probably off on a drunk, they said), that he was aloof and morose and that his shabby appearance (left) was a disgrace. It was suggested to Lincoln that he remove the General from command. "No, I can't do it," said Lincoln. "I can't spare this man. He fights." Grant kept on fighting. By capturing Vicksburg (July 4, 1863) he broke Confederate control of the Mississippi and split the South in two. Over thirty thousand troops surrendered. His plan, said Lincoln in elation, was to "hold on with a bulldog grip and chew and choke as much as possible." When Grant came to Washington in March, 1864, at Lincoln's request, he was, according to Richard Henry Dana, "a short, round-shouldered man, in a very tarnished . . . uniform . . . no station, no manner . . . and rather a scrubby look withal."

As general-in-chief of all the armies of the United States, Grant hammered away at Lee in Virginia, with Richmond as his goal. This incompleted sketch (right) of Lincoln and his son Tad with Grant was drawn by Winslow Homer at City Point, Virginia, a few days before the President entered Richmond. Homer, a special war artist for *Harper's Weekly,* later became America's finest water colorist.

W. H . 65.

"I met you once before, General Lee, while we were serving in Mexico, and I have always remembered your appearance," said Grant when the two met at Appomattox Court House (below) on April 9, 1865. They then sat down and Lee heard Grant's generous terms: the Confederates were permitted to keep their horses and return home, and the officers could retain their side arms. Grant then ordered 25,000 rations to be turned over to Lee's starving army.

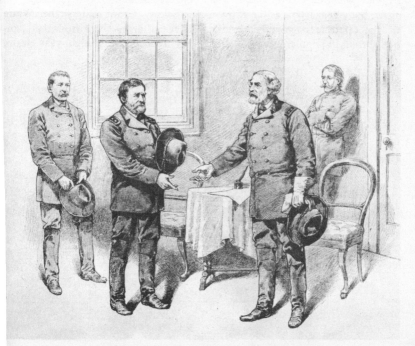

March 4, 1869.
A GIANT AMONG THE PIGMIES.

Grant was indeed a giant among pygmies when he was inaugurated in 1869, but a year later (as the cartoon on the opposite page indicates) he had shrunk in popular esteem.

Grant knew nothing about politics. He had voted only once in his life in a presidential election—as a Democrat for Buchanan in 1859—and was without party affiliation when the Republicans sought him out. At first he could not decide whether to accept their overtures. His salary as general was $25,000. The Presidency offered the same amount, provided he were elected and re-elected. But, he wondered, what would happen to him after that? At length he yielded and the Republicans unanimously nominated him on the first ballot. He was elected by a popular majority of but 309,584 votes out of 5,716,092 cast.

Bitter Andrew Johnson refused to ride in the carriage with Grant to the inauguration and did not attend the ceremonies.

Below, Grant enters the White House after his drive from the Capitol to begin his eight-year term.

The giant began to look like a pygmy when he chose for his seven-man Cabinet two favorites from his little home town of Galena, Illinois, and another man unfit for high office. The country gasped at the selections, but gasped more at the scandal that soon followed.

This was the attempt by two stock manipulators, Jay Gould and Jim Fisk, to corner the nation's gold market. Gould bribed Grant's brother-in-law, A. R. Corbin, to supply inside information from the White House. Fisk, working with Gould on the scheme, entertained the President and tried to convince him that the United States Treasury should not sell gold on the exchange (it was traded like a stock in New York's Gold Room). In the belief that Grant was fixed, the two schemers began buying and drove the price from 132 to 163½. At last aware of the plot, Grant ordered the Treasury to sell four million dollars' worth of gold. The corner collapsed, creating a panic on "Black Friday,"

March 4 1870.
A PIGMY AMONG THE GIANTS.

September 24, 1869 (below). Many legitimate Wall Street brokers were ruined. Although the guileless Grant was innocent, he was accused of criminal incompetence in allowing himself to be mixed up in the affair.

The above picture was drawn by Cadet Grant at West Point in 1842. Grant always had a great love of horses. Once, when asked if he liked Washington, he replied that he'd like it better if it had a good road on which he could drive fast horses.

Grant had new stables built on th White House grounds (above) an kept several fast-stepping horses. O time in Washington he was arreste for speeding, but the charge was n pressed. (Unless a president submi voluntarily he cannot be arrested Left, Grant and Robert Bonner ta a spin on Harlem Lane, New Yor

Nellie Grant, the President's only daughter (he had three sons), was married at the White House on May 21, 1874, to Algernon Sartoris, a handsome young Englishman she had met on a steamer. Society columns of the day overspilled with descriptions of the event—of the gifts on display valued at $75,000, of Nellie's white satin wedding gown with Brussels point lace which cost $5,000, and the great floral wedding bell in the gas-illuminated East Room. Upstairs the President lay on his bed with his face buried in a pillow, sobbing like a child.

During the summers Grant took his family to Long Branch, New Jersey, then the fashionable watering place of the country. His cottage (below) "is a very tasteful and elegant bit of summer architecture," said *Harper's Weekly*.

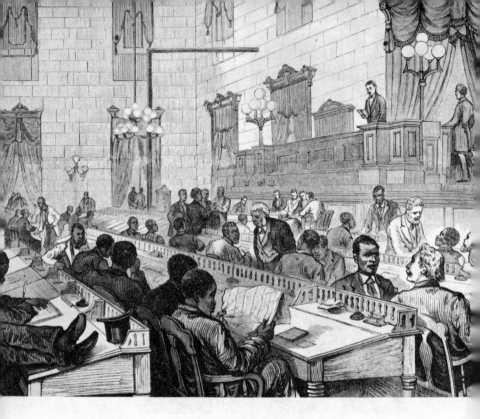

President Grant supported the radical Republicans with the result that northern political adventurers

(carpetbaggers) rushed south and joined the white riffraff (scalawags) to exploit the Negro vote. That they did is evidenced in the above picture of a meeting of the South Carolina legislature in 1876, then composed of seventy-eight whites and sixty-two Negroes. (In the first reconstruction legislature after the war there were eighty-seven colored and forty white.) The conservative white people looked upon this corrupt and incompetent "black and tan" rule with deep disgust and fought it with every weapon available. One weapon was the Ku Klux Klan (left), a terrorist organization which resorted to murder, arson, and assaults upon both whites and Negroes. Many of the outrages were committed against unoffending citizens.

"I CANNOT TELL THE TRUTH."

Grant gave up the bottle when he became president, but his political enemies continued to portray him as a drunk. On this page he is shown (above) as a threadbare Bowery bum doing a tipsy jig; as a befuddled inebriate (above, right) whose coat of arms is emblazoned with cigars and a bottle of liquor; and (right) sodden, in the arms of a squaw. This cartoon was in reference to his humane policy toward the Indians. Many were Grant's weaknesses. He was impressed by rich men, and was a poor judge of character. But liquor was not one of his failings as president.

THE PEACE POLICY OF OUR NOBLE PRESIDENT.

America celebrated its hundredth birthday in 1876 and proudly looked itself over. From a narrow strip of land along the Atlantic coast the nation now spread to the Pacific and had a land area more than three times its original size, a population increase of some forty million. The

thirteen stars on the flag that Washington carried into battle now numbered thirty-eight. America in 1876 had become the world's greatest single source of food and one of the leading industrial powers in the world. No other country could boast such growth or progress in the material conditions of life.

Reflecting the hundred years of progress are the illustrations on these two pages which appeared on the occasion of the Philadelphia Centennial Exhibition, 1876. The left sides of the pages represent conditions in the country in 1776; the right sides, the advances made in one hundred years. Thus, on the bottom of this page (left), we see the half-famished farm animals of a century before in contrast (right) to the sleek, well-fed stock of 1876.

"Custer's Last Stand" took place at the Little Big Horn River, Montana, on June 25, 1876, when a Sioux war party led by Chiefs Crazy Horse and Gall annihilated some 260 United States cavalrymen to score the greatest victory of Indian warfare.

Little Charlie Ross (above) was picked up by two men in a wagon in front of his Germantown, Pennsylvania home on July 1, 1874, and was never seen again. The country was incensed by the kidnaping, the first for ransom (twenty thousand dollars).

In the heyday of the cow country, after the Civil War, untold thousands of cattle were driven north out of Texas every year.

"STONE WALLS DO NOT A PRISON MAKE"—Old Saw.

Crooked Tammany leader "Boss" Tweed (above) pilfered many millions of dollars out of New York City's treasury in the seventies. At last convicted, he was released after a short term. Convicted again, he died in jail in New York.

The only photograph of Grant without a beard (left) was the result of a misunderstanding. When his wife requested that his profile be photographed so that she could have a cameo made, the President thought she wanted the actual lines of his face shown. He reluctantly shaved and had his picture taken.

Grant's closing years were tragic. After a trip around the world, following his second term, he formed a Wall Street brokerage firm. His unscrupulous partner, borrowing huge sums on Grant's name, plunged the firm into bankruptcy. Penniless, in disgrace and dying of cancer of the throat, the old General began to write his *Personal Memoirs* so that he could pay his debts and leave something for his family.

Below, doctors consult at his New York home.

In the summer of 1885 Grant was taken to Mount McGregor in up-state New York where he occupied a cottage with his family. His *Memoirs* finished (the two-volume work brought $450,000 to the family), the General could no longer talk, and made his wishes known in a feeble scrawl (above).

He died on July 23, 1885, and was buried in a temporary tomb (below, left) on Riverside Drive, New York. The permanent tomb, dedicated in 1897 (below), bears the inscription, "Let Us Have Peace."

RUTHERFORD B. HAYES 1822–1893
President 1877–1881

The above daguerreotype of Rutherford Birchard Hayes and his wife, Lucy, was made on their wedding day, December 30, 1852, at Cincinnati, Ohio. At that time the thirty-year-old Hayes was a successful lawyer in Cincinnati; his wife, younger by nine years, was a graduate of the Cincinnati Wesleyan Woman's College.

The young woman who was to become known throughout the land as "Lemonade Lucy" because as First Lady she refused to serve alcoholic beverages in the White House was, like her husband, serious-minded, deeply religious and strait-laced.

Hayes was a transplanted New Englander of Puritan stock whose parents migrated to Ohio in 1817. Five years later Rutherford was born at Delaware, Ohio—a posthumous child, like Andrew Jackson before him. Unlike Jackson, however, young Rutherford never knew poverty. The widow Hayes was left well off, and

with the help of her bachelor brother, into whose house she moved after her husband's death, Rutherford was sent to a New England academy, Kenyon College in Ohio, and to Harvard Law School. Rutherford's path was smooth and untroubled. He never got into any scrapes or had any wild oats to sow, or did anything wrong at all. A Puritan will always find something to reproach himself for, however, as this entry in his diary while he was at Harvard demonstrates: "Welladay, more faults to cure . . . Trifling remarks, boyish conduct, etc., are among my crying sins. Mend, mend! . . . I am quite lame from scuffling, and all my fingers stiffened from playing ball. Pretty business for a law student."

The author of those words turned out to be a dashing, fearless officer all through the Civil War. He was wounded in action, led a reckless charge at the Battle of Winchester and emerged from the war a brevet major general. The people of Ohio admired him so much that they elected him to Congress before the war was over, but he stayed in

the army until Lee's surrender. In Congress he made a reputation for honesty and efficiency, and later was thrice elected governor of Ohio. Moving quietly on the political scene, Hayes was entered as Ohio's favorite son in the Republican convention at Cincinnati in 1876. Much to the country's surprise, he defeated the favorites in the race for the nomination.

TILDEN.   **HAYES.**

OF THE TWO EVILS
CHOOSE THE LEAST.

The general cynicism of the times is reflected in this pre-election card. Both the Democratic candidate, Samuel J. Tilden of New York, and Hayes were honest, capable, and beyond reproach in public and personal life. But many people, disgusted by the scandals of Grant's administration, the corrupt carpetbag rule in the South, the spoils system, and the infamous Tweed Ring in New York City, could not help but think that most politicians were crooks, or at best pawns in the hands of the industrial giants and barons of Wall Street.

The country had something to be cynical about in the 1876 election. On the morning after Election Day the newspapers announced the results: Tilden the winner, 4,300,590 popular votes and 196 electoral votes to Hayes' 4,036,298 and 173. Clearly a Democratic victory, but the Republicans would not concede. They claimed that in three southern states Tilden carried (Louisiana, South Carolina and Florida), Negroes had been unlawfully kept from going to the polls. Had they been allowed to vote, Hayes would have been elected. Republican leaders and Southern Democrats met and made a deal: The three states would throw their electoral votes to Hayes, thereby giving him the election 185 to 184, provided that federal troops would be withdrawn, and the states would be allowed to control their own affairs. The bargain made, it was kept. An Electoral Commission created by Congress decided in favor of Hayes on March 2, 1877, just fifty-six hours before the inauguration. (Below, the announcement of Hayes' election.) Hayes had nothing to do with the stolen election.

Soon after she entered the White House, Mrs. Hayes gave notice that no liquor or wines would be served while she was First Lady. The edict was greeted by jeers mingled with some applause, notably by the Women's Christian Temperance Union, which presented the above portrait to Mrs. Hayes. (It still hangs in the White House.) A story got around that at diplomatic dinners the servants, unknown to Mrs. Hayes, were supplying rum-filled oranges to the guests. Washington wags called this stage of her dinners the "Life-Saving Station." The President had his little chuckle about this. The joke was "not on us but on the drinking people," he wrote in his diary. "My orders were to flavor (the oranges) . . . with the same flavor that is found in Jamaica rum. This took! There was not a drop of spirits in them." Besides banishing alcohol, Lemonade Lucy brought egg-rolling to the White House lawn.

A SQUATTER ON THE "ROCKS"

WHO OUGHT TO BE EVICTED AS SOON AS POSSIBLE.

WHEN HAYES WAS PRESI-DENT: One of the most widely read authors was Horatio Alger, Jr. whose more than one hundred books, based on the "rags to riches" theme, influenced a generation of American youth.

A wild West variety show in the 1870s.

America's most disliked man of the gaslit era was Jay Gould (above) who made millions in stock manipulations. Once, fleeing New York from the law with six million dollars in cash, he chortled to his companions "Nothing is lost, boys, save honor."

The song below was composed in honor of New York's Elevated Railroad. In the '70s trains ran from 12 to 15 miles per hour.

One of the first out-of-door demonstrations of the telephone was given by its inventor, Alexander Graham Bell (shown right, talking into the instrument), in Salem, Massachusetts, on March 15, 1877. As Bell spoke to his assistant in Boston, reporters in both cities recorded the conversation; later compared notes to prove that there had been no deception. A few months later Bell spoke to the President over thirteen miles of wire. Fascinated, Hayes promptly installed a phone in the White House.

When the Pullman Company introduced the "President," a "Hotel Car," in 1877 (below) the event was hailed in the press: "Here is a luxurious home with every comfort. A wheeled hotel!"

In April, 1878, Thomas A. Edison (right), a thirty-one-year-old inventor who had recently been granted a patent on his phonograph, was invited to the White House to give a demonstration to the President. It must have been a successful one for he did not leave until 3:30 A.M. A year later the young wizard demonstrated the first commercially practical electric lamp (right) at Menlo Park, New Jersey.

167

JAMES A. GARFIELD 1831–1881
President 1881

James Abram Garfield, the somberly dressed, scowling figure on the opposite page who looks like the villain of a cloak-and-dagger play, was in real life totally unlike his appearance in this camera portrait. He was a blue-eyed blond with yellow hair and yellow beard and was genial, easygoing and warmhearted. He was one of the few scholarly men of the Presidency. A lover of poetry and the classics, he wrote passable verse and could read and write Latin and Greek. (He used to entertain his friends by simultaneously writing Latin with one hand and Greek with the other.)

Born of poor parents in a shanty (above, right) at Orange, Ohio, he was the last log cabin president. His father died when the boy was two and young Jim went to work at ten, driving horses and mules on the towpath of a canal (above). His rags-to-riches career is typical of the Horatio Alger stories of the Victorian era. In Alger fashion the faultless lad thrashed the bully of the towpaths, worked hard and scraped together enough money to put himself through school and college. After his graduation from Williams College in 1856

he returned to Ohio and married his boyhood sweetheart, Lucretia Rudolph. At this time he was president of Hiram Institute at Portage, Ohio, and professor of Latin and Greek. He found time to study law and was admitted to the bar just before the outbreak of the Civil War.

Garfield went off to war as a lieutenant colonel of Ohio volunteers and performed so brilliantly in the field that within a year he was a brigadier general—at thirty the youngest one in the army. Like Hayes, he was elected to Congress while still in the army, but unlike Hayes he resigned his commission (on the advice of Lincoln) and went to Washington. There he served in the House for the next eighteen years.

When the Republicans met at Chicago in 1880 the fight for the nomination was between James G. Blaine of Maine and ex-President Grant, recently returned from a trip around the world. (Hayes had disqualified himself by announcing that he would not seek re-election.) As ballot after ballot was cast it was apparent that neither Grant nor Blaine could win. In order to break the deadlock the delegates compromised on the dark-horse candidate, Garfield, who was nominated on the thirty-sixth ballot.

Garfield defeated the Democratic candidate, Winfield Scott Hancock, by the slim majority of 9,464 votes out of more than 9,000,000 cast. The above view of the "Grand Military and Civic Procession" at the inauguration on March 4, 1881, is from the dome of the Capitol. Visitors in those days used to climb there for a full view of Pennsylvania Avenue stretching between the Capitol and the White House.

The old bitterness between the North and South was becoming a thing of the past when Garfield took office. Hayes had withdrawn the last of the federal troops, carpetbaggery had ended after ten weary years and white home rule had returned to the southern states. An incident during the inaugural procession symbolized the growing harmony when a group of ex-Confederate soldiers broke through the crowd on Pennsylvania Avenue, waved the Union flag and cheered Garfield and retiring President Hayes (above).

Right: a guided tour of sight-seers in the rotunda of the Capitol. For many years in the last century the great circular hall sheltered a bazaar where peddlers sold a variety of wares including stoves, buggy whips, snake oil, mousetraps, kitchen utensils and pianos.

On July 2, 1881, less than four months after Garfield's inauguration, a demented office seeker named Charles J. Guiteau fired two shots at the President as he stood with Secretary of State Blaine in the Baltimore and Potomac depot in Washington. One shot grazed the President's arm; the other entered his back fracturing the spine. The assassin was quickly collared and taken off to jail. In the weeks that followed, as the President lay suffering in the White House, well-wishers brought a variety of medicines.

ONE OF THE BULLETS.

GUITEAU'S ENGLISH BULLDOG PISTOL.

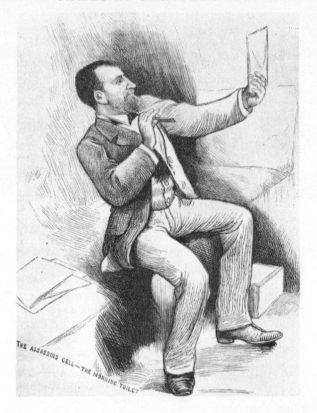

THE ASSASSINS CELL—THE MORNING TOILET

"WILL YOU GIVE THIS TO THE PRESIDENT?"

COLLECTION OF QUACK MEDICINES AND APPARATUS.

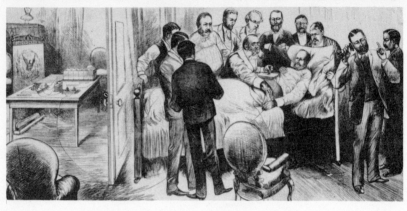

Alexander Graham Bell was summoned to the White House to find the exact location of the bullet by means of his induction-balance device (above). The President lingered on through the hot summer. On September 6 he was moved in a special train to the seaside town of Elberon, New Jersey, where his wife (left) constantly attended him and prepared all his meals. Garfield seemed to be recovering until September 19 when he awoke with a chill and grew progressively weaker. He died that night at ten-thirty.

Below: the body is returned to Washington.

As the train passed through Princeton the student body paid tribute to the President by strewing flowers on the railroad track (above).

On November 14, 1881, in the Supreme Court of the District of Columbia, the trial of Guiteau began. He was defended by his brother-in-law, George Scoville, who argued that Guiteau was insane. The government contended that he was of sound mind, had long planned the murder and had acted for the sake of revenge. (Guiteau, seeking a consulate in France, had once gotten in to see Garfield, but nothing had come of the brief interview, nor of the steady stream of letters he subsequently sent to the President.) During the ten-week trial Guiteau acted like a madman most of the time. He shouted, constantly interrupted the Court and delivered long, incoherent speeches. On January 25 the trial ended. It took the jury only an hour to find that Guiteau was sane and guilty.

On June 30, 1882, the bearded, forty-year-old man was led to the gallows in the Washington jail before a crowd of more than two hundred people, many of whom had paid fancy prices to see the execution. On the platform Guiteau recited a poem he had written for the occasion and kept on talking after the black hood had been pulled over his face.

CHESTER A. ARTHUR 1830–1886
President 1881–1885

Chester Alan Arthur, a machine

politician from New York, looked
like a president—he was over six fee
tall, courtly, and always stylishl
dressed—and to everyone's surpris

acted like one from the moment he took the oath of office. (Above, Arthur is sworn in at his Lexington Avenue home, New York, at 1:30 A.M., September 20, 1881. Two days later the oath was formally administered in Washington.)

The son of a Baptist preacher, Arthur was born in Fairfield, Vermont, on October 5, 1830. He put himself through Union College at Schenectady, New York, studied law and moved to New York City where he was admitted to the bar in 1853. After the Civil War, during which he was quartermaster-general of the state, Arthur became a henchman of Roscoe C. Conkling, Republican boss of New York, and organized a Grant-for-President Club. In gratitude, Grant in 1871 appointed him collector of the port of New York, a lucrative post that gave him control over considerable patronage. Although he was not personally corrupt, Arthur so openly used his power to fatten the New York ma-

chine that President Hayes removed him from office in 1880. That year Arthur and Conkling went to the Chicago convention to support Grant for a third term. When Garfield was nominated, the victorious Republicans, wishing to appease the powerful Conkling, allowed him to name the second place on the ticket. He chose Arthur, never dreaming of course that his crony would be in the White House in less than a year, conducting a reform administration. Overnight Arthur changed from a minor politician to an efficient and honest executive who believed that his first duty was to his country. He broke with Conkling, supported the Civil Service Law, which did much to remedy the evils of the spoils system, prosecuted Republicans accused of post-office graft, and vetoed a pork-barrel rivers-and-harbors bill. Arthur lost machine support and the renomination because of his courageous reforms, but he won the gratitude of the American people.

In the above cartoon from *Puck,* ex-President Grant says to the horrified Arthur, "Here are some friends of mine who never refuse office."

Grant's "friends" were his discredited Cabinet members (Belknap, Robeson and Williams), his dishonest secretary Babcock, and the corrupt Republican politicians Murphy and Shepard. Nothing like this happened, for Arthur refused Grant political favors and broke with him.

A more truthful portrayal (left) shows the President as a fop. Arthur had a passion for fashionable clothes, had them made to order by a New York tailor and was groomed by his personal valet. He installed the first tiled bathroom in the White House. He spent large sums for flowers, and never forgot to place a bouquet every day before the photograph of his dead wife, Ellen Herndon Arthur.

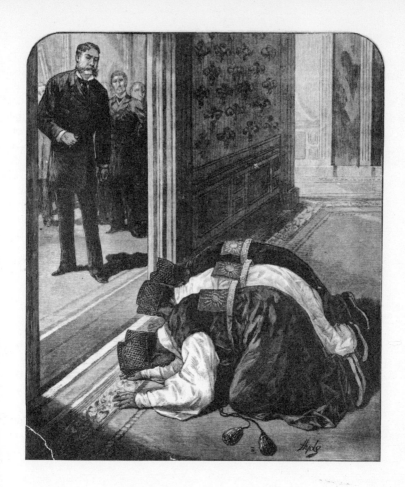

In 1882 Congress passed the first Chinese Exclusion Act which barred Chinese laborers from entering the country for ten years. Since the Gold Rush days of 1849 some 300,000 Chinese had poured into California and it was feared that if the unchecked immigration continued, the Pacific Coast would be swamped by coolies.

In the same year the United States signed a treaty of commerce and friendship with Korea as an independent state. As a result of these negotiations Korea established an embassy in Washington. In September, 1883, an "Envoy Extraordinary," headed by Min, Yong and Ik, the nephews of the King of Korea, came to New York to be presented to President Arthur, who was then stopping at the Fifth Avenue Hotel. At the entrance of the presidential suite the three envoys, richly dressed in oriental court robes, gave a deep salaam (above), then entered the suite in single file and bowed low to everybody.

WHEN ARTHUR WAS PRESIDENT: Brooklyn and Manhattan were linked upon the opening of the great Brooklyn Bridge on May 24, 1883 (left). At a cost of fifteen million dollars and twenty workmen's lives, it had taken thirteen years to build. The 1,595-foot bridge was designed by John A. Roebling, a German immigrant who manufactured the first wire rope in America. President Arthur and Grover Cleveland, Governor of New York, led the first walk across the bridge.

BERGHIANA.

HUMANE HENRY'S NEW YEAR'S DREAM OF A HIGHLY IMPROVED HEAVEN.

Six days after the opening, a great panic took place when someone in the crowd of strollers screamed that the bridge was giving way (below). People fought to get off and got jammed together on the stairways. Twelve were crushed to death, some forty injured.

A much-abused man by the cartoonists and jokesters of the day was Henry Bergh (above), founder of the American Society for Prevention of Cruelty to Animals. Many people looked upon the humane Bergh as a crank and a meddler.

Above, immigrants at Castle Garden, New York Harbor. In the 1880s over five million newcomers entered the United States.

Panic swept Wall Street in May, 1884 (above), when brokers learned of the sixteen-million-dollar failure of Grant & Ward. Ferdinand Ward, the General's crooked partner, later got a ten-year sentence. Grant was exonerated. After the crash his personal assets amounted to less than two hundred dollars.

The buffalo had almost disappeared by the 1880s. Above, the last relic—a heap of bones to be shipped for fertilizer.

The dime novel was considered an abomination by parents of the last century. The principal publisher was Erastus F. Beadle, whose firm put out hundreds of books between 1860–1897. They are now prized by collectors and often exhibited in libraries.

GROVER CLEVELAND 1837–1908
President 1885–1889 (First Term)

Stephen Grover Cleveland (he dropped the "Stephen" at an early age) was the only president to be re-elected after leaving the White House, the first Democratic president since Buchanan, and like Buchanan came to the White House a bachelor.

"Grover the Good," as the Demo-

IT'S MINE?

crats called him, had little formal education, no wealth or family prestige, was not physically attractive—he weighed 260 and was bull-necked—and had no gift of oratory. But he had an immovable, stubbornly honest character. Of great independence and courage, he was successively sheriff of Erie County, New York, mayor of Buffalo and governor of the state. As sheriff he personally hanged two murderers rather than give the unpleasant task to his deputies. He was called the "veto mayor" because of the sledge-hammer blows he delivered to Buffalo's political grafters. As governor he refused to do the bidding of Tammany, the New York City Democratic machine, and won the approval of the better element of both parties.

"We love him for the enemies he has made," said Edward S. Bragg, a Wisconsin delegate, in his speech nominating Cleveland at the Democratic convention in 1884. It was an allusion to the opposition of Cleveland by Tammany. The phrase took hold and became a campaign slogan.

It was the dirtiest campaign in United States history. The Republican candidate, James G. Blaine, was branded a grafter for allegedly accepting over one hundred thousand dollars from a railroad for his services while he was in Congress. The Republicans responded by revealing that Cleveland had once sired an illegitimate child. When faced with the charge, Cleveland wired his frantic campaign managers, "Whatever you say, tell the truth." The truth was that he had once formed an "illicit connection with a woman and a child had been born and given his name." Cleveland admitted this although there was no proof that he was the father since other men had been involved.

Above, Cleveland lands the Presidency as the defeated Blaine stalks off.

The picture above, a *carte de visite,* was taken of Cleveland in 1864 when he was twenty-seven years old and assistant district attorney of Erie County, New York. Cleveland did not join the Boys in Blue in the Civil War. By the terms of the Conscription Act of 1863, a man eligible for the draft could avoid service by furnishing a substitute, or paying a commutation of three hundred dollars. With two brothers in the army and a mother and two sisters to support, Grover decided to stay home. He paid $150 to a substitute who went off in his place.

Below, following the inaugural ceremonies on March 4, 1885, the President and Chester Arthur review the parade from a stand in front of the White House.

Cleveland was the hardest-working man in Washington. He stuck to his desk regularly until two or three o'clock in the morning, going over the details of his job. "He would rather do something badly for himself than have somebody else do it well," said Tilden. Cleveland did few things badly. He vetoed a pension grab for war veterans, improved the civil service while his partisans clamored for the spoils of office, and opposed the high tariff.

Cleveland was the first and only president to be married in the White House. His bride was Frances Folsom (right), the daughter of his law partner and closest friend in Buffalo, Oscar Folsom. When Folsom was suddenly killed, being thrown from a buggy, Cleveland acted as executor of the estate and looked after the widow and her eleven-year-old daughter. For many years Cleveland saw a great deal of the two, but no one suspected that he had more than a paternal interest in Frances. When she graduated from Wells College he wrote her offering marriage, and the engagement soon followed. At the time (1886), she was a tall, graceful, dark-eyed young woman of twenty-two. The President was forty-nine.

The marriage took place in the Blue Room on June 2, 1886, with fewer than forty people present. The service had been revised and con-densed by Cleveland and the word "obey" was omitted. As the ceremony closed, a salute of twenty-one guns thundered from the navy yard and all the church bells in the city rang out.

WHEN CLEVELAND WAS PRESIDENT: The Apache Indians of the Southwest headed by Chief Geronimo were the scourge of the white settlers in that region. After a sensational campaign (1885–1886) Geronimo was captured by General Crook. The chief is shown (left) as he was brought into San Antonio with thirty-two bucks and squaws. Geronimo, with members of his tribe, eventually settled as farmers in Oklahoma. He wrote his life story in 1906, died in 1909.

On October 28, 1886, the bronze Statue of Liberty was unveiled at Bedloe's Island, New York Harbor. The 225-ton statue, designed by the French sculptor, Frederic Bartholdi, was presented to the United States by the French government.

At a meeting called by anarchist labor leaders at Haymarket Square, Chicago, on May 4, 1886, a bomb thrown by an unknown person exploded among the policemen, killing seven and injuring many others. As a result, the movement for the eight-hour day was set back for a generation.

The sod house (right) was the most common abode in the treeless Nebraska plains in the land boom of the seventies and eighties. Using matted turf as bricks, a man could build a weather-tight house in ten days with no tool but a spade. It was cooler in summer, warmer in winter than a house of lumber.

The great blizzard of '88 (March 11–14) was accompanied by high winds and bitter cold, caused many deaths and isolated several towns and cities along the Atlantic coast. In New York City (below), where more than twenty inches fell, all transportation ceased, resulting in a food panic. The city's only communication with the outside world was via commercial cable.

"The Last Yankee. Unrestricted immigration and its results—a possible curiosity of the Twentieth Century," was the title of this *Leslie's* 1889 cartoon (below).

BENJAMIN HARRISON 1833–1901
President 1889–1893

Benjamin Harrison, grandson of our ninth President, William Henry Harrison, drifts through the four-year interlude between the two Cleveland administrations as a cautious, frigid, unimaginative little man (five feet, six inches) who was content to sit in the White House and let Congress run the country. The men who put Harrison in office—the rich manufacturers seeking high-tariff benefits —contributed the largest campaign fund in history up to that time and did not expect their man to shape the policies of the government, as Cleveland had done. He did not disappoint them. His administration was more responsive to the "special interests" than any since Grant's. Unlike Grant, however, he was free from scandal and his regime was an honest one.

Harrison's career is as uninspiring as the man himself. He was born at North Bend, Ohio, graduated from Miami College and studied law for two years in Cincinnati. In 1853 he married Caroline Scott (above), a preacher's daughter. The couple moved to Indianapolis where he took his first job as court crier for $2.50 a day. Later he became city attorney, court reporter, and when the Civil War came he was commissioned colonel of an Indiana regiment and rode with Sherman. Returning to Indianapolis after the war, he was nominated as the Republican candidate for governor, but met defeat. In 1881 the Indiana legislature elected him to the United States Senate where he served one term without distinction. Defeated for re-election, he left Washington in 1887, convinced that his political career was behind him. In two years he was president.

Life in the White House with the Harrisons was, like his administration, plain and uneventful. There was little entertaining, no glamorous dinners. The systematic President never

varied his daily habits: breakfast at eight followed by a half hour of prayer by the entire family closeted in one room, a one o'clock lunch, early dinner and early to bed. The new electric lights, installed in 1891, baffled the Harrisons. They let the lights burn all night in the halls and parlors, fearing that if they turned them off they would get a shock. They were extinguished by the White House electrician when he came on duty in the morning. For a long time the Harrisons did not use the lights in their bedrooms, and were even fearful of pushing the electric bell buttons.

He went to the war at the first call for men.

Whilst Cleveland was a bar-room lounger.

His bravery in the field was noted and conspicuous.

Whilst Cleveland paid a substitute to fight for him.

He stands between the workman and Free Trade.

Whilst Cleveland attempts to smash our Industries.

During the Harrison-Cleveland campaign of 1888 the above cartoons appeared in *Judge,* a humorous weekly devoted to the Republican cause. Political cartoonists pulled no punches in those days, were often unfair and vicious. In the top four cartoons Harrison (left column) is shown as a war hero, Cleveland, a saloon loafer and slacker. (Cleveland was a moderate drinker, occasionally frequenting saloons in his early Buffalo days, but was attracted by food rather than liquor. His war record is noted on page 184.) Harrison was a high-tariff man (bottom two cartoons) while Cleveland stood for lowering duties on manufactured goods, but he was not a free trader. Cleveland's stand on the tariff was instrumental in his defeat for re-election—although he received more popular votes than his opponent.

The strongly Democratic weekly, *Puck,* delighted in showing the diminutive Harrison almost lost under the big hat of his grandfather, William Henry Harrison. In this cartoon, below, published in 1890, the President appears to be of such small stature that Uncle Sam has to peer through a microscope in order to see him. Though small in many ways, Harrison was an honest middle-of-the-roader. His administration enacted the highest protective tariff thus far reached (the McKinley Tariff Act), a pension act for Union war veterans which soon depleted the Treasury's enormous surplus, a silver bill (increasing the government's purchase of silver), and the Sherman Anti-Trust Act which was ineffective and practically became a dead letter. None of these measures originated with the President himself.

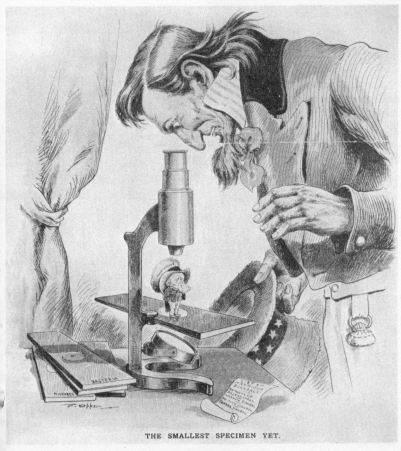

THE SMALLEST SPECIMEN YET.

WHEN BENJAMIN HARRISON WAS PRESIDENT: The country suffered its worst peacetime disaster when Conemaugh Dam, twelve miles above Johnstown, Pennsylvania, broke on May 31, 1889, and a runaway lake swept down the valley submerging the city and outlying towns. About 2,205 lives were lost and the damage was estimated at ten million dollars. In a deep irregular valley, Johnstown got the full force of Lake Conemaugh which, before the dam broke, was two and a half miles long and one hundred feet deep in places.

America's fistic hero in the eighties and nineties was John L. Sullivan (below) who fought the last bare-knuckle bout at Richburg, Mississippi, on July 8, 1889, defeating Jake Kilrain in seventy-five rounds (two hours and sixteen minutes).

The last pitched battle between Indians and white men (above) took place at Wounded Knee Creek, South Dakota, on December 29, 1890, when the Seventh Cavalry rushed a Sioux encampment and slaughtered over two hundred men, women and children in a few minutes. The massacre was the army's terrible revenge for Custer's defeat in 1876. The Battle of Wounded Knee completed the conquest of the Indian and marked the end of an epoch.

WORKMEN CANNONADING THE BARGES.

WORKMEN ATTACKING THE BARGES.

SURRENDER OF THE PINKERTON MEN.

PINKERTON'S CAPTIVES ON THEIR WAY TO PRISON.

Joseph Jefferson III (above) delighted American audiences from 1859 to 1904 by playing the role of Rip Van Winkle.

One of the first automobiles was this one-cylinder, 4-h.p. Duryea which was made in Springfield, Massachusetts, in 1893.

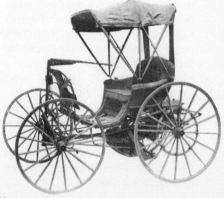

The first great industrial strike, the Homestead (Pennsylvania) strike of 1892, was a result of wage cutting by the Carnegie Steel Company. Some three hundred armed Pinkerton men surrendered to the strikers after a battle on July 6 in which ten people were killed (above). The strike was broken in six months.

GROVER CLEVELAND 1837–1908
President 1893–1897 (Second Term)

When Mrs. Cleveland departed from the White House on March 4, 1889, an hour or so before the Harrisons moved in, she said to the staff, "Take good care of all the furniture and ornaments in the house . . . for I want to find everything just as it is now when we come back again. We are coming back just four years from today."

Four years later to the day (March 4, 1893) in a sleet storm, Cleveland drove up Pennsylvania Avenue by the side of the man who had taken the Presidency from him (above) and was now returning it to him. Never before had a once-defeated president been able to enjoy such a triumph. With 277 electoral votes against Harrison's 145, his victory was the most decisive since the re-election of Lincoln. In a complete Democratic sweep the party controlled both houses of Congress as well as the Presidency for the first time since the Civil War.

"Grover! Grover! four more year of Grover!

Out they go, in we go; then we'l be in clover."

So went the victors' song, but ther was little clover in the fields fo Grover, or for the country. A de pression was already under way du to a number of causes, among then the depletion of the nation's gold re serve during Harrison's administra tion. A world-wide business depres sion further darkened the clouds.

Hard times were probably in evitable, but as usual the party i power was held responsible—as th cartoon from *Judge* on the opposit page illustrates. How could anyon but a moron be glad that he vote for Cleveland, asked *Judge* in 1894 when the greatest number of men i United States history were unem ployed, hundreds of banks had failed railroad construction had almos ceased, agricultural prices were at th bottom, mercantile failures amounte to $347,000,000 and ruin had visite many thousands of honest, toilin people.

194

THE GREATEST CURIOSITY OF THE NINETEENTH CENTURY.

The Hoffman House Bouquet Cigar
Foster-Hilson Company Makers

Advertisers in the last century made free use of national celebrities, and even the President and First Lady, to promote their products. In the above picture, for example, Cleveland and other well-known figures of the time stand in the lobby of New York's Hoffman House, unwitting endorsers of a brand of cigar. Far left is United States Senator David B. Hill; in the foreground Cleveland chats with Chauncey M. Depew, president of the New York Central Railroad. Others distributed about the lobby are: "Buffalo Bill" Cody, Tony Pastor (creator of American vaudeville), and at the counter (far right) Professor Herrman, the magician, and actor Nat Goodwin.

The Sparks' Medicine Company offered with their compliments this porcelain tray (left) bearing a picture of the First Lady.

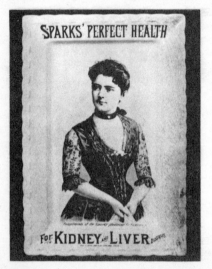

SPARKS' PERFECT HEALTH

FOR KIDNEY AND LIVER DISEASES

WHEN CLEVELAND WAS PRESIDENT: The Chicago World's Fair (Columbian Exposition) ran from May through October, 1893, and attracted more than 21,000,000 people. Almost every country in the world was represented. Among the innovations: the Ferris Wheel and the 250,000 electric lamps lighting the grounds.

In 1894 J. S. "General" Coxey led an "army" of about three hundred unemployed men from Ohio to Washington seeking work and federal aid.

The first movie studio (below), called the Kinetographic Theater, was built for Edison in 1893 at West Orange, New Jersey. Here the inventor made movies, synchronized the action with his phonograph and thus produced what was later known as the "talkies."

A wage cut by the Pullman Company in 1894 resulted in a strike called by socialist Eugene Debs, who ordered a boycott of all trains entering Chicago with Pullman cars. Federal troops were used to quell riots.

Copyright
by
E. Chickering.
'91. Boston.

WILLIAM McKINLEY 1843–1901
President 1897–1901

William McKinley, the third martyred President within a space of thirty-six years, was the last Civil War veteran to become president. A gentle, dignified man of great kindness and sincerity, he was one of the few who frankly sought the Presidency (in 1888 and 1892) and finally achieved his goal.

The great issue of 1896—on the surface, at least—was gold versus

silver: the Democratic stand for unlimited coinage of silver to expand the currency against the Republican pledge to maintain the gold standard. Inflation against sound money. Underlying it all was a deeper conflict—the agrarian West and South opposed to the industrial East; the "toiling masses" against the "special interests," as the Democrats put it.

In an exciting campaign that at times reached the fanaticism of the Crusades, William Jennings Bryan, the Democratic candidate, toured the country four times and made more than six hundred speeches. McKinley, whose campaign was ably handled by multimillionaire Mark Hanna of Ohio, stayed at home in Canton and spoke from his front porch. The candidates characterized the issues—the conservative, calm McKinley stressing prosperity and "the full dinner pail"; the thirty-six-year-old Bryan, "The Boy Orator of the Platte," attacking the trusts and Wall Street as he whirled eighteen thousand miles around the country.

He failed to convince the country of the virtue of his panacea, however. McKinley was elected by a landslide, receiving 271 electoral votes to Bryan's 176.

No more devoted or more pathetic couple than the McKinleys (above) ever dwelt in the White House. When Ida Saxton, the pretty and well-educated daughter of a Canton banker, married McKinley in 1871 she had every reason to look forward to a life of normal happiness. But within three years she lost her mother and two baby daughters. The calamities so shattered her nervous system that she developed epilepsy. For the rest of her life she could not tell from minute to minute when she would fall unconscious. With a patience and kindness rarely seen, McKinley shielded her, insisted that she go everywhere with him and responded to her every summons. When he was not working he took no recreation but remained at her side, trying to make her existence more livable.

"IF WILLIE IS A GOOD BOY, AND MINDS PAPA AND NURSIE, THEY WILL TRY TO LET HIM KEEP THE PRETTY HOUSE UNTIL HE IS EIGHT YEARS OLD."

BACK TO THE FARM.

Little boy McKinley taking orders from the trusts and Mark Hanna was the view taken by the Hearst papers in 1896 (above, left). While McKinley did represent the business interests, he was in no sense the puppet of Mark Hanna, who twice successfully managed his campaigns. The President was re-elected in 1900 by a greater majority than before, defeating Bryan by 292 electoral votes to 155.

Bryan as seen by *Judge* in 1900 (above) skulks off to his Nebraska farm carrying the full dinner pail of Republican prosperity. At this time a greater abundance of gold in the country had all but killed the silver issue and Bryan's campaign, following our war with Spain, was based on anti-imperialism. He predicted that America's acquisition of islands and rise to a world power would lead to national decay, similar to that of ancient Rome. In 1908 Bryan made his last hopeless fight for the Presidency.

Left, McKinley's second inaugural, March 4, 1901. The President was then at the apex of his popularity.

WHEN McKINLEY WAS PRES-
IDENT: The Boxer Rebellion in
China (1900), aimed against foreign
nations, resulted in the murder of
many missionaries and other foreigners. To relieve the beseiged
Americans and Europeans in danger
of massacre at Peking, the United
States and five other nations sent relief troops, and the uprising was sup-
pressed. Over a $300,000,000 indem-
nity was levied upon China, and
many Boxers were executed. Right,
Li Hung Chang, Chinese executioner,
with a collection of Boxer heads.

Carry Nation (below), Kansas
temperance agitator, became a coun-
try-wide, notorious figure from 1900
on as a saloon wrecker. Wielding a
hatchet, Carry took joy in destroying
liquor, furniture and fixtures in estab-
lishments that sold intoxicants.

Finley Peter Dunne (above), Chicago humorist and creator of the
Irish saloonkeeper-philosopher "Mr.
Dooley" and his friend "Mr. Hen-
nessy," was at his prime in the late
nineties and early 1900s. His books,
written in Irish brogue, were widely
quoted.

LOOK OUT, BOYS!
THE WEATHER MAN PROGNOSTICATES A CYCLONE FROM KANSAS.

201

The first action of the Spanish-American War took place on May 1, 1898, when Commodore George Dewey (above, directing maneuvers from the flagship *Olympia*) steamed into Manila Harbor with four cruisers and two gunboats to engage the Spanish fleet. Within a few hours the accurate and devastating fire of the Americans silenced all shore batteries and annihilated the Spanish fleet. The Americans did not lose a ship or a man and had only eight men slightly wounded. The Spanish lost eight ships, 167 men killed, 214 wounded.

McKinley did not want the war, but the blowing up of the United States battleship *Maine* in Havana Harbor, causing the death of 260 of her officers and crew, brought forth the vengeful cry "Remember the *Maine!*" and the war was on. In the shortest, most unique and one-sided war America ever fought, not a single reverse was suffered and not a soldier, gun, color, or an inch of ground was captured by the enemy.

Ha! ha! " It didn't hurt a bit," Spain says.—*Los Angeles Times*.

The cartoon (right) shows Uncle Sam making the final extraction—the surrender of Santiago, following the destruction of the remnants of the Spanish fleet. On July 26, Spain asked for peace terms.

The signing of the peace protocol (below) took place in the White House on August 12, 1898. In this picture the President observes the signing by (left to right) William R. Day, Secretary of State, and Jules Cambon, the French ambassador. Spain gave up Cuba and ceded Guam, Puerto Rico and the Philippines to the United States.

BUFFALO  EXPRESS.

ESTABLISHED 1846. Vol. LVI. No. 85. · · · BUFFALO, N.Y., SATURDAY, SEPTEMBER 7, 1901. · · · TEN PAGES.

THE PRESIDENT SHOT AT THE EXPOSITION.

On September 6, 1901, at Buffalo's Pan-American Exposition, a young anarchist named Leon Czolgosz, who had a revolver concealed in a handkerchief, took his place in the reception line filing past the President. As he came face to face with McKinley he fired twice through the handkerchief. One bullet struck McKinley in the breastbone; the other ripped through his abdomen. As the wounded President was caught and supported by his aides, he whispered to his secretary, "My wife—be careful, Cortelyou, how you tell her—oh be careful."

BUFFALO EXPRESS.

ABLISHED 1846. Vol. LVI, No. 218.　　BUFFALO, N. Y., SATURDAY, SEPTEMBER 14, 1901.　　TWELVE PAGES.

RESIDENT M'KINLEY IS DEAD--
HIS SOUL FREED AT 2.15 O'CLOCK

McKinley died eight days after the shooting. "I thought it would be a good thing for the country to kill the President," said Czolgosz in his cell. He was electrocuted forty-five days after McKinley's death. Mixed with the sorrow of the people was a wave of humiliation that such a terrible record of assassination could exist in America.

Below, a soldier boy stands guard over a photo of the departed President—a typical bit of sentiment of the times.

Above, the ambulance that took the President from the Exposition to the Buffalo home where he and his wife were staying.

Below, the .32-calibre Iver Johnson revolver used by the assassin, and the handkerchief that covered it.

THEODORE ROOSEVELT 1858–1919

President 1901–1909

Theodore Roosevelt was the youngest man to become president, the wealthiest (up to his time), the most popular since Andrew Jackson, and by far the most athletic, dynamic, colorful and adventurous. No shrinking violet was our twenty-sixth President. "I took the Canal Zone and let Congress debate," he said. "I and my people thank you," read the cable

to the President of Peru. A true extrovert, yet of great intellectual power, he wrote some 150,000 letters while he was in the White House and over thirty books during his lifetime. The wide range of subjects in his books reveals the man's many-sided character: a history of the War of 1812, *The Deer Family, Through the Brazilian Wilderness, Life of Oliver Cromwell, The Winning of the West, History as Literature, African Game Trails,* and so on. No other president ever led such a strenuous or diversified life.

The line from Browning, "I was ever a fighter," should stand as Roosevelt's epitaph, for that was the keynote of his career. His first fight began in the house where he was born on East Twentieth Street, New York (above), when he was nine years old. Frail of body and asthmatic, he fought for physical power in a gymnasium his father had constructed on the third floor of the house. He fought at Harvard in boxing tournaments (as a lightweight)

and as a young assemblyman he fought the corrupt legislature of New York. His battles continued, both physical and political, as a Dakota rancher, New York police commissioner, colonel in the Spanish-American War, governor of New York, and president.

Perhaps the most important battle he ever fought was one with himself, which he lost but which proved to be the turning point of his career. It concerned the Vice-Presidency. When it was offered him in 1900 by "Tom" Platt, Republican boss of New York, Roosevelt replied, "I would a great deal rather be anything . . . than Vice-President." Nine days before the convention he wrote, "I will not accept under any circumstances and that is all there is about it." But when Roosevelt was convinced that his refusal might mean the election of Bryan, he reluctantly accepted the nomination. Having lost the battle with himself, he said, "I do not expect to go any further in politics."

Roosevelt in the eighties (when these photographs were taken) was, according to one newspaper reporter, ". . . short and slight and with an ordinary appearance, although his frame is wiry and his flashing eyes and rapid nervous gestures betoken a hidden strength. . . . Although of the old Knickerbocker stock, his manner and carriage is awkward, and not at all impressive." The Old Guard in the New York Assembly saw him as a Harvard dude and a "googoo"—a derisive term applied to one devoted to "good government."

A few months after his graduation from Harvard in 1880, Roosevelt married Alice Lee, shown on the left in the above picture. They went to Europe, where young Teddy climbed the Matterhorn to equal the feat of two boastful Englishmen who had recently made the climb. (Above, left: Roosevelt in his mountain-climbing outfit.) After his wife's death in 1884 Roosevelt (left) went west and spent two years working his ranch on the banks of the Little Missouri River in Dakota. Working on the round-up and riding for days he won the strength of body he had set out to gain.

When the war with Spain came, Roosevelt quit his job as assistant secretary of the Navy and helped organize the Rough Riders, a picturesque cavalry regiment composed of cowboys, Indians and eastern college football players. The famed charge of the Rough Riders up San Juan Hill, Cuba, where Roosevelt led his men in the face of heavy fire, is shown in the above illustration. It was drawn by Frederic Remington, who was in the engagement. At a barbed-wire fence at the crest of the hill Roosevelt sprang off his horse and plunged on, his men following. The Spaniards were put to rout, thus placing the American army on high ground overlooking Santiago.

The colorful Rough Riders captured the imagination of the country, and when Roosevelt returned from Cuba he found himself a popular hero. So great was his fame that this letter (left) bearing only a crude likeness was delivered to him at his home in Oyster Bay, Long Island.

Twenty-eight Pages.

BUFFALO 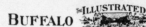 ILLUSTRATED EXPRESS.

Printed by Electric Power from Niagara Falls.

D

PART 2—PAGES 9 TO 26—Vol. LVIII No. 36.   BUFFALO, N. Y., SUNDAY, SEPTEMBER 15, 1901.   PRICE FIVE CENT

ROOSEVELT QUICKLY SWORN IN AS PRESIDENT-- M'KINLEY'S BODY TO LIE IN THE CITY HAL

On September 13, 1901, Roosevelt was in the heart of the Adirondacks when a guide brought him a telegram to the effect that McKinley was dying. He hastened to Buffalo, arriving there thirteen hours after the President's death, and took the oath of office. On the McKinley funeral train leaving Buffalo, Mark Hanna said, "Now look, that damned cowboy is President of the United States."

"ISN'T IT JUST POSSIBLE THAT I'M OVERDOING THIS BUSINESS?"

At the turn of the century the American people were greatly concerned over the growing power of the trusts, or monopolies, which were threatening the economic life of the country. Trust magnates believed that they were a privileged class beyond the reach of restraint. But they were destined to a rude awakening for Roosevelt, under the banner of a "square deal," fought the monopolistic combinations which were suppressing free competition.

Roosevelt's many-sidedness appealed to all manner of men. He was, as Secretary of State John Hay wrote: "Of gentle birth and breeding, yet a man of the people . . . with the training of a scholar and the breezy accessibility of a ranchman; a man of the library and a man of the world; an athlete and a thinker; a soldier and a statesman . . . with the sensibility of a poet and the steel nerve of a rough rider." The mass of Americans agreed. Roosevelt was elected in 1904 by an unprecedented majority.

His greatest service to the cause of peace was performed in 1905 when, through his initiative, Russian and Japanese delegates met at Portsmouth, New Hampshire (above), and agreed upon a peace that ended the war between those two nations.

Roosevelt received the Nobel Peace Prize for this achievement.

Below: Teddy in Panama, 1906. He was the first president to leave the shores of the United States.

211

The above picture was taken at "Sagamore Hill," Roosevelt's Oyster Bay home, which was the summer capital of the United States for seven seasons. Left to right: Kermit, Archie, the President, Ethel, Mrs. Roosevelt (Edith Kermit Carow), Quentin and (standing) Theodore, Jr. Not shown is Alice, Roosevelt's daughter by his first wife.

On the opposite page the President is depicted by cartoonist John McCutcheon of the Chicago *Tribune* pursuing his creed, "The Strenuous Life."

PRESIDENT ROOSEVELT IS RESTING AT OYSTER BAY

First he chops down a few trees.

Then takes a cross-country canter.

And a twenty-minute brisk walk.

After which he gives the children a wheel-barrow ride.

He then rests for a moment

By which time he is ready for breakfast.

WHEN ROOSEVELT WAS PRESIDENT: The Wright brothers of Dayton, Ohio, made the first successful airplane flight on December 17, 1903, at Kitty Hawk, North Carolina. This picture (left) shows Orville at the controls at the moment of launching (the flight lasted twelve seconds) with his brother, Wilbur, at the right. A newspaper reporting the event next day headlined the story: "NO BALLOON ATTACHED TO AID IT." Roosevelt paid $25,000 to the Wrights in 1909 for a plane, thus beginning the United States Air Force.

After many unsuccessful attempts to reach the North Pole, Admiral Robert E. Peary (below) sailed north on the 184-ton *Roosevelt* in 1908 for a final try. Then fifty-three, his life's ambition was realized on April 6, 1909, when he reached the Pole.

Anxious Boatman: NOW, MARY, WHAT-EVER HAPPENS, DON'T MOVE YOUR HEAD, OR WE'LL CAPSIZE!

This cartoon from *Life* (1909) pokes fun at the enormous wide-brimmed hat then in vogue. With it came the flaring, gored skirt that swept the street on all sides.

When the above cartoon appeared in 1903, showing the saintly John D. Rockefeller about to swallow the globe, the Standard Oil king had amassed some $300,000,000 and his fortune was increasing daily.

Jolted by severe earthquakes on April 18, 1906, the city of San Francisco suffered greater devastation when a fire broke out and burned for three days (above). In the quake and fire 452 people were killed; property damage was over $350,000,000.

The Great Train Robbery (right) was the first moving picture to tell a story. Produced by the Edison Company in the fall of 1903, the epoch-making thriller was filmed in New Jersey and directed by Edwin S. Porter, the first man to use the "cut-back." The film was tinted yellow for the dance-hall scene, bluish green for the woods. One of its actors, G. M. Anderson of Brooklyn, later achieved stardom in Western roles as "Broncho Billy."

Roosevelt left the presidency in March, 1909 (above), and sailed for Africa with his twenty-two-year-old son Kermit, to hunt big game. Teddy carried with him a rabbit's foot given to him by his friend, John L. Sullivan. The charm worked, for the two hunters killed over five hundred animals and birds, including seventeen lions and an assortment of rhinos, elephants, hippopotami, and giraffes. Upon emerging from the jungle in April, 1910, he visited Rome, where he sought an audience with the Pope. The Pope agreed to see him, provided that Roosevelt would not call on some Methodist missionaries in Rome. Roosevelt had no intention of doing this, but he declined to submit to the Pope's conditions and the interview did not take place. "An elegant row," said Teddy of this episode. He went on to Paris, Berlin (where he reviewed the Kaiser's troops), Christiania (for the Nobel Prize), Oxford and London, returning home in June, 1910.

GOOD BOY!

Upon his return Roosevelt found the Republican party disrupted by factional strife and headed for disaster. "My hat's in the ring," he said to his followers, who bolted the Republican convention in 1912 to form the Progressive party. "I feel as fit as a Bull Moose." The phrase gave the new party the unofficial name of the Bull Moose Party. On October 14, 1912, while speaking in Milwaukee, he was shot in the breast by a crazed assailant. "I have just been shot," he said calmly. "But it takes more than that to kill a Bull Moose . . . The bullet is in me now, so that I cannot make a very long speech . . . I want you to understand that I am ahead of the game anyway. No man has had a happier life than I have led; a happier life in every way."

In a three-cornered election in 1912, Roosevelt polled over four million votes, but was defeated by Woodrow Wilson, the Democratic candidate. A year later he led an expedition into the jungles of Brazil where he explored nine hundred miles of an unknown river, since named the Río Teodoro by the Brazilian government. When the war with Germany came Roosevelt offered again to raise a division of troops, but Wilson refused his consent.

Above, "The Long Long Trail," J. N. (Ding) Darling's famous drawing, which appeared shortly after Roosevelt's death on January 6, 1919. This is the reverse of the original drawing which showed T.R. with his right hand holding the reins, his left waving his hat.

"And in his time a man plays many parts."
Shakespeare.

Cowboy   Historian   Police Commissioner   Naval Secretary   Rough Rider   Governor of New York   Vice President   President   Peacemaker   Mighty Hunter all the time

WILLIAM HOWARD TAFT 1857– 1930
President 1909–1913

"Big Bill" Taft, our largest President, stood six feet, two inches, weighed over three hundred pounds, and was the only man in American history to hold the two highest offices in the land—the Presidency and the Chief Justiceship of the Supreme Court. The good-natured, jovial Taft had no taste for politics, was lacking in executive force and probably would have been better off if he had never hearkened to the lure of the Presidency. Although he was brilliant (he stood second in a class of 121 at Yale), honest and more successful than many presidents, he was at heart a judge. He spent the first twenty years of his career, save two, in courts as a law officer and judge, and his ambition was to attain the Supreme Bench.

"I do not want my son to be president," said his mother. "His is a judicial mind and he loves the law." His wife (Helen Herron), however, opposed a judicial career as being a "fixed groove." The picture above of Taft and his wife driving from the 1909 inauguration shows who won the contest between the two ladies.

Taft left his chosen career at the urging of President McKinley in 1900 to head the newly formed Philippine Commission. In his new role at Manila the big, genial fat man treated the Filipinos with an openness and sincerity they had never before experienced from foreign rulers. He spoke warmly of them as "my little brown brothers." Twice while he was governor of the Philippines, President Roosevelt offered Taft a berth on the Supreme Court and twice Taft refused because he felt that his first duty was toward the Filipinos.

A disturbing report that Taft's health was failing caused Secretary of War Elihu Root to send a cabled inquiry. Taft replied that his health was fine, that he had just ridden twenty-five miles on horseback. "How is the horse?" cabled Root. Taft's great tonnage inspired many jokes and no one enjoyed them more than he did. Arthur Brisbane said that Taft looked "like an American bison, a gentle, kind one."

When Root resigned his Cabinet post, Roosevelt offered Taft the

vacant office. The War portfolio appealed to him because it would permit him to administer to the Filipinos. On February 1, 1904, he took the oath of office as secretary of war.

These two cartoons illustrate the shattering of the Taft-Roosevelt friendship which shocked the country and brought defeat and humiliation to both men.

Below (from *Puck,* 1909), Teddy joyfully presents his good friend Taft, the "Crown Prince," to the American public. Below, right (from *Life,* 1912), Taft and Roosevelt, now enemies, strain against each other in a bitter fight for the Republican nomination. What caused this unhappy quarrel?

Toward the end of Roosevelt's administration the President was at the peak of his popularity. He was only forty-nine and would have liked the Presidency for another four years, but he had given his word not to run again. "Under no circumstances will I be a candidate for or accept another nomination," he had publicly stated. As the 1908 convention drew near Roosevelt determined to turn the nomination over to Taft, "the most lovable personality I have ever come in contact with." Having made the decision, Roosevelt dedicated himself to his loyal friend. He engineered his nomination, campaigned vigorously for his election and saw

him through to a smashing victory over William Jennings Bryan (321 electoral votes to 162). "Taft will carry on the work substantially as I have. His policies, principles, purposes and ideals are the same as mine," said Teddy.

But the genial Taft was no Roosevelt. The minute Teddy was gone the standpatters took the tiller from Taft's uncertain hands and steered a reactionary course. Roosevelt returned to find his party disrupted, many of his reforms cast aside and the Taft administration steadily losing prestige.

Thus ended the long friendship. At first there was a coolness between the two. Then came the open break when Roosevelt sought the Republican nomination in 1912. Teddy's anger carried him to extremes. Taft, he bellowed, was "useless to the American people" . . . "disloyal to every canon of decency and fair play." Taft did not reply in kind but his supporters did. A pamphlet distributed in Chicago when the egotistical Teddy was there read: "At three o'clock Thursday afternoon Theodore Roosevelt will walk on the waters of Lake Michigan."

The Taft administration was one of strife between the standpatters and the insurgents, or progressives, and little was accomplished. Taft, however, created several presidential "firsts" during his regime. He became the first president to set foot on foreign soil when he visited President Diaz of Mexico in 1909. He was the first golfing president (right), the first to open the baseball season by tossing out a ball, the first to have a government car (an electric runabout, a gasoline-powered sedan, and a White steamer). He was the first president to draw a salary of $75,000. (Prior to Grant, who received $50,000, the salary was $25,000.)

Taft left the White House in 1913 with no regrets. As he departed he said to President Wilson, "I'm glad to be going. This is the lonesomest place in the world." He found contentment as professor of law at Yale (below) for nine years and as chief justice of the Supreme Court from 1921 until his death in 1930.

WHEN TAFT WAS PRESIDENT: Glenn H. Curtiss (above) won a prize of ten thousand dollars by flying from Albany to New York City on May 29, 1910. The 143-mile flight took two hours, fifty-one minutes. He made two stops en route for gas and repairs.

On October 1, 1910, the Los Angeles *Times* building was dynamited, killing twenty-one. The McNamara brothers, strike leaders, pled guilty and were sentenced to San Quentin.

In the pre-World War I era when Enrico Caruso was at the height of his fame, he drew this caricature of himself as Pagliacci.

AT LAST.
Old Earth—" What a relief to have that spot scratched. It's been itching for fifty thousand years."

The Cook-Peary fight over who discovered the Pole was settled in Peary's favor.

Above, four musical comedy favorites as they appeared in *Hokey Pokey* in 1912. From left to right: Lillian Russell, Joe Weber, William Collier and Lew Fields.

To thousands of farm families in the Taft-Wilson era the most prized possession was the Model-T Ford, shown (right) on the porch of an imperiled farmhouse during a flood at Shaw, Mississippi, in 1913. Henry Ford began to mass-produce the Model-T in 1908 and by 1913 his assembly lines were turning out about one thousand cars a day. In 1914 when half a million flivvers were on the road, Ford announced that he would pay a minimum wage of five dollars per eight-hour day to his thirteen thousand employees.

WOODROW WILSON 1856–1924
President 1913–1921

Thomas Woodrow Wilson, who dropped his first name while a boy, as did Stephen Grover Cleveland before him, came to the Presidency by an unusual path. He was president of Princeton University, had never held political office, and had never taken more than a theorist's interest in politics when, at fifty-three, he was called off a golf course one afternoon in 1910 to receive the nomination for the governorship of New Jersey. Two years later he was elected president of the United States.

Wilson, like Jefferson and Theodore Roosevelt, was among the most literate of the presidents. He was a historian of recognized authority whose books were used as texts in schools, and had been a professor of jurisprudence and political economy in three colleges. He was cold, aloof and often arrogant, but he was not all intellect. At Wesleyan University in Connecticut he coached the football team for two years. He liked vaudeville better than *Hamlet*. He write scores of limericks. He was the most popular lecturer at Princeton where he gained the reputation of being both interesting and weighty.

As president of Princeton, Wilson made headlines by trying to abolish the exclusive eating clubs on the campus, and although he failed he was lauded as a champion of the underdog. New Jersey politicians began to wonder if this fighting professor wouldn't be a good vote-getter, even if he was a Ph.D. Wilson accepted the nomination for governor with the understanding that if he were elected he would govern, and not the machine politicians. The Democratic bosses of New Jersey smiled at such simplicity and laughed aloud when the professor sat down in the governor's chair. But he soon let them know who was the boss and put through a series of reforms such as the state had never before known.

"A Presidential campaign may easily degenerate into a more personal contest and so lose its real dignity. There is no indispensable man," said Wilson in his speech accepting the Democratic nomination on August 7, 1912. Thus did Wilson state his political philosophy and his personal platform. He refused to take part in the public brawl between Taft and Roosevelt and the people liked him for it. He was always suavely polite to his two opponents, and even praised Taft for his patriotism and integrity. When Roosevelt was shot, Wilson halted his campaign until his opponent recovered. The country admired this gesture of sportsmanship. By limiting himself to the realm of ideas and avoiding personalities, the dignified and sensible Wilson got results. The conviction spread that this clear-thinking professor knew what he was talking about. The election was no upset. Although he received fewer popular votes than Taft and Roosevelt combined, Wilson carried forty out of the forty-eight states, polling 435 electoral votes to his opponents' 96.

Below, the Wilson family in 1912. From left to right: Eleanor, Mrs. Wilson, the President, Margaret and Jessie. The President's wife died in the White House on August 6, 1914. In December of the following year Wilson married Mrs. Edith Bolling Galt.

Taft was glad to dispose of the "Mexican situation" by handing the troublesome infant to his successor in 1913. Wilson was confronted with a civil war in Mexico which kept the Rio Grande country in a constant state of turmoil. When the bandit chief "Pancho" Villa raided Columbus, New Mexico, in 1916 and killed fifteen Americans, Wilson ordered General John J. Pershing to invade Mexico and get Villa. The expedition, which cost about $150,000,000 was unsuccessful. American troops kept watch along the Rio Grande until 1920.

DON'T MIX IN A FAMILY QUARREL, UNCLE

As a youthful scholar at Johns Hopkins University working on his thesis for a Ph.D., Wilson conceived a philosophy of government which he put into practice when he went into politics. It was, basically, that a governor or president should lead, rather than be led by a political machine or by Congress. A president should act more like a prime minister, less like a "mere department" isolated from Congress. His theory had worked well when he put it to the test as governor of New Jersey, and he intended to continue it as president. The country was electrified when Wilson, at a special session of Congress a month after his inauguration, walked in and delivered his message in person. Not since John Adams had a president addressed Congress. In a brief, pithy address Wilson summarized his policy with pointed recommendations of things to be done. The statement was received with a thunderous ovation. Soon Congress was grinding out the greatest number of reform laws that had ever been passed in an equal length of time. Among them were: The Federal Reserve Act which gave the nation the control of its own money for the first time; a lower tariff revision; a more forceful antitrust law; a child-labor law; and the creation of the Federal Trade Commission, designed to prevent large corporations from using unfair methods of competition. Wilson's first administration was crowded with accomplishments, most of which remain in force today.

The cartoon above illustrates America's attitude toward the quarreling European powers when war broke out in August, 1914. Like Wilson, the country felt that it was none of our business.

England's scorn for Wilson and the American people because of our reluctance to enter the war is illustrated in this cartoon (above) from *Punch*, October 18, 1916. Entitled "Bringing It Home," Wilson says, "What's that? U-boats blockading New York? Tut! tut! Very inopportune."

Wilson's early attitude toward the war was to turn his back upon it, to snub it. "There is such a thing as a man being too proud to fight," he said in a speech on May 10, 1915. The phrase "too proud to fight" was later hurled back at him with contempt. The campaign for his re-election was waged mainly on the slogan, "He kept us out of war." But the war could not be snubbed.

Germany's proclamation of unrestricted submarine warfare caused Wilson to go before Congress on February 3, 1917 (below), and advise a severance of diplomatic relations. On April 2 he again addressed Congress. This time he called for war. To go into a war in whose origin we had no part was a fearful thing to do, he said, but it was necessary "to make the world safe for democracy."

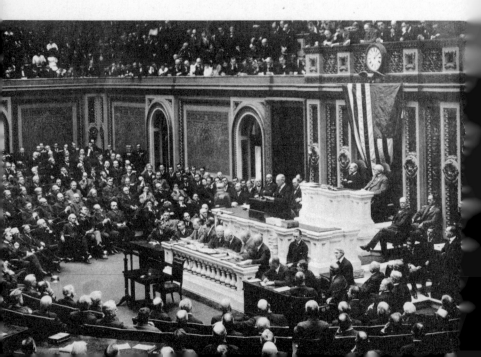

To many men Wilson was distant and "schoolmasterly," a thinking machine. Women, especially attractive women, did not find him so, however. He responded to their admiration, was gay and warm in their company and liked to have them about. He was dependent upon them to an extraordinary degree. Before he was president, Wilson's home was a fortress of femininity. His three adoring daughters and his devoted wife continually pampered and petted him, and looked upon him as their lord and master. Less than a year after his first wife's death Wilson fell in love with Mrs. Galt, the handsome forty-three-year-old widow of a Washington jeweler. The President, then fifty-eight, became an ardent wooer. He sent her flowers daily, had a private wire installed between her home and the White House and put aside all save the most important affairs of state to be with her. They were married on December 18, 1915.

Above, the President and his wife drive back from the Capitol, March 4, 1917. This was the last time a carriage was used at an inauguration.

Early in December, 1918, Wilson sailed for France to attend the Paris Peace Conference. In a triumphant tour of France, England and Italy the President received tremendous ovations. He was hailed as "the people's man," the apostle of a new order. He did not ask for land or money, the usual prizes of war; he sought only a secure peace, a League of Nations to make future wars impossible.

Below, left: Wilson with President Poincaré of France; below, right: with England's King George V.

230

The Peace Conference was a prelude to the final work—the Treaty of Versailles, which was signed at three o'clock on the afternoon of June 28, 1919, in the great Hall of Mirrors in the Palace of Versailles. At that moment the first World War came to an end.

In this picture of the signing, Wilson sits between United States Secretary of State Robert Lansing (with his hand to cheek) and Georges Clemenceau, Premier of France. On Clemenceau's left is Lloyd George, Britain's Prime Minister.

Governor Calvin Coolidge of Massachusetts (far right in the above picture) greeted the Wilsons when they landed in Boston on February 24, 1919. The President came home

to consult leaders of both parties about the peace treaty, stayed only two weeks, then returned to France. In July he returned for good. At this time the Treaty of Versailles, which included the League of Nations Covenant, had been signed, but it had yet to be approved by the United States Senate. The League was Wilson's great dream. It was the heart of the treaty and he supposed it unthinkable that it would be rejected. But to his horror he found that there was much objection to it. In an effort to win support Wilson took a "swing around the circle" (left) and appealed directly to the American people.

Against the advice of his physician, Admiral Grayson, Wilson started out on his speech-making tour on September 3, 1919. At sixty-three the President had aged noticeably. One side of his face twitched and he was continually in a state of nervous exhaustion—in turn despondent and irritable. Yet he was determined. "There will come sometime . . . another struggle in which, not a few hundred thousand fine men from America will have to die, but many millions . . . to accomplish the final freedom of the peoples of the world," he warned a St. Louis audience. At Pueblo, Colorado, he suffered a stroke and the rest of the trip was canceled. With drawn blinds, the train switched around the city of Wichita, Kansas, where he was scheduled to speak, and went directly to Washington. The physical breakdown of the President was hastened by the Senate's rejection of the Treaty in November. Below, one of the last photographs of the President, taken shortly before his death on February 3, 1924.

WHEN WILSON WAS PRESIDENT: The Panama Canal, begun in 1904, was formally opened to commerce on August 15, 1914. The engineer chiefly responsible for the completion of the fifty-mile-long ditch was Colonel George W. Goethals. Without the aid of army surgeon William C. Gorgas, however, the canal might never have been completed. As chief sanitary officer, Gorgas did notable work in suppressing yellow fever, thus making the digging of the canal possible.

Below, the celebration in Wall Street, November 7, 1918, of the false armistice, released prematurely by the United Press. Four days later came the announcement of the real armistice and an even greater nationwide celebration.

The *Oscar II*, chartered by Henry Ford (below, at left), sailed from Hoboken, December 4, 1915 (without Ford) for Norway with a party of peace lovers determined "to get the boys out of the trenches by Christmas." The "Peace Ship," a squirrel cage of do-gooders and freeloaders, failed in its purpose.

"Freed from Demon Rum," the country went dry in 1919 under a wartime prohibition act to continue until the end of mobilization. But the Eighteenth Amendment replaced it in 1920. The United States was constitutionally a Sahara for fourteen long years.

In 1920 Charlie Chaplin made *The Kid* (above), one of his greatest pictures, in which he appeared as the tramp foster father of a small boy played by Jackie Coogan.

Prior to the first World War a trend called "feminism"—the emancipation of women from old taboos —was taking place in the country. One of its manifestations was the woman's suffrage movement. By 1912 women had the right to vote locally in ten states and had partial suffrage in twenty-one others. Not until the Nineteenth Amendment went into effect in 1920, however, could women everywhere vote in a presidential election. The Amendment added some nine million women voters to the seventeen million who already had the right to vote in local elections.

WARREN G. HARDING 1865–1923

President 1921–1923

Warren Gamaliel Harding, Ohio's seventh President, was a successful small-town businessman, genial and easygoing, who wanted more than anything else to be liked by his fellow men. He was a typical "Main-Streeter" of the 1920s. In Marion, Ohio, where he lived most of his life, he was the owner of the local newspaper, director of a bank, a lumber

company and the telephone exchange. He played the cornet in the Marion band. He chewed tobacco. He was a "joiner." Popular with the home-town folks, he was extremely kind and sympathetic. In thirty-six years as publisher of the Marion *Star* he never dismissed a single employee. He was softhearted to a fault and could not believe that there was evil in any man. He never learned to say no. "It is a good thing I am not a woman. I would always be pregnant. I cannot say no," he once told some Press Club friends.

In 1891 when he was twenty-six and on his way to becoming Marion's leading citizen, he married Florence De Wolfe Kling (shown above with his father, Dr. George T. Harding). Some six years older than her husband, Florence Kling was the daughter of the town's leading banker. She was the pusher of the family, always ambitious for her husband's success. Harding called her "the Duchess" and often followed her advice, which was sometimes based on her consultations with an astrologer.

Harding looked like a president. He was superbly handsome, big-framed, with large, wide-set eyes, and he had a pleasant resonant voice. Of the many people who were impressed by the Harding personality, one was Harry M. Daugherty, a sharp-eyed Ohio politician. The first time the two met, Daugherty saw in the big genial man the possibilities of a president. He became Harding's mentor and master-minded his political career as he rose from state senator to United States senator. "I found him sunning himself, like a turtle on a log," said Daugherty of his protégé, "and I pushed him into the water."

The 1920 Republican convention shaped up as a fight between General Leonard Wood and Frank O. Lowden, Governor of Illinois. Behind them came the other possible candidates: Senator Hiram Johnson of California and Nicholas Murray Butler, President of Columbia University. Harding's name was far down the list but Daugherty had a plan he had long been working on.

Foreseeing a deadlocked convention, Daugherty told a reporter what he thought would take place. "After the other candidates have failed . . . the leaders, worn out and wishing to do the very best thing, will get together in some smoke-filled hotel room about 2:11 in the morning. Some fifteen men, bleary-eyed from lack of sleep, and perspiring profusely with the excessive heat, will sit down around a big table. I will be with them and present the name of Senator Harding. When that time comes, Harding will be selected." Daugherty proved to be an amazing prophet. The event came off almost exactly as he had predicted, even to the bleary-eyed leaders in the smoke-filled hotel room at 2:11 A.M. Harding was stunned to learn that he had been chosen. He did not want the Presidency. He only wanted to remain in the Senate for the rest of his life.

In an uninteresting campaign conducted from the front porch of his Marion home (above), Harding stressed a return to "normalcy." He defeated the Democratic candidates James M. Cox and his running mate Franklin D. Roosevelt.

As president, Harding's small-town habits did not change much. He played poker most every night with his cronies, played golf (mid 90s) and took in baseball games (below, shaking hands with Babe Ruth). His Cabinet contained some able men, and some obviously unfit for public office. Daugherty, his Attorney-General, was soon under fire for irregularities, as this cartoon (right) indicates, and was later brought to trial. The jury was unable to agree after sixty-six hours of deliberation. Harding's corrupt Secretary of the Interior, Albert B. Fall, who accepted a $100,000 bribe for leasing United States oil reserves to private interests, was convicted and sent to prison. There were other scandals. The trusting, unsophisticated President had no part in them. He simply did not know what was going on.

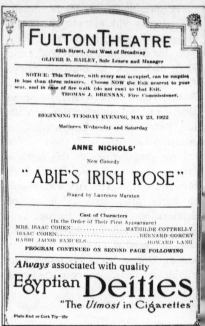

WHEN HARDING WAS PRESI-DENT: The radio became a fact (above). In 1920 there were five thousand receiving sets in the United States, over two and one-half million four years later. Harding was the first president to speak over the air (at the Minnesota State Fair, September, 1920).

Above, opening night program of *Abie's Irish Rose,* a play described by reviewers as "something awful." It stayed on the boards for five years, five months, playing 2,327 perform-ances—a record up to that time.

In the presence of 100,000 people, Chief Justice Taft on May 30, 1922, presented the Lincoln Memorial to President Harding, who accepted it in behalf of the American people. One of the most beautiful buildings in America, its walls are surrounded by thirty-six Doric columns of white marble, each one representing a state at the time of Lincoln's death. In the center space within is a colossal statue of Lincoln.

In 1923 when this picture was taken of a Ku Klux Klan parade in Youngstown, Ohio, the organization numbered some four million people, most of whom were dedicated to the hatred of Jews, Catholics, Negroes, immigrants, the League of Nations and pacifism. Revived in 1915 by William J. Simmons, a circuit-rider of the Methodist Episcopal Church from Atlanta, Georgia, the Klan became a powerful force in southern and midwestern states in the midtwenties and at one time had political control of seven states.

Another phenomenon of the zany twenties was the dance marathon, introduced to America on March 31 in 1923 by Alma Cummings who established a record of twenty-seven hours of continuous dancing. This picture (left) shows Joie Ray, famed miler and long-distance runner, with his partner, Alice King, during a contest at Newark, New Jersey. The craze lasted well into the 1930s.

Emile Coué (right, pointing) came to the United States from France in 1923 with his cure-all autosuggestion system, organized a clinic and treated thousands of gullible patients.

CALVIN COOLIDGE 1872–1933
President 1923–1929

Calvin Coolidge, Vice-President of the United States, went to bed at nine o'clock as usual on the night of August 2, 1923, at his father's home in Plymouth, Vermont, where he was enjoying a short vacation. At half-past two in the morning he was awakened and told that President Harding was dead. Coolidge hastily dressed and went downstairs to the parlor which was lighted by a flicker-

ing kerosene lamp. There he was addressed for the first time as "Mr. President," the words being spoken by his father. A copy of the Constitution was found and Calvin took the oath of office administered by the elder Coolidge, a notary public (above).

Thus did the famed "Coolidge Luck" persist. Had Harding died twenty-four hours later, Coolidge would have taken the oath in the home of a multimillionaire friend he was planning to visit. But luck gave him a perfect setting—the old family farmhouse in the Vermont hills, his mother's Bible on which he took the oath, the bespectacled farmer-father. The simple ceremony appealed to the American people and was in perfect character with the tight-lipped, industrious Vermont farm boy with the nasal twang. "Calvin," said his father, "could get more sap out of a maple tree than any of the other boys around here." Cal got votes out of the people as he did sap out of the trees from the beginning of his career. On the way up he held more elective offices than any other president (nineteen) and was only once defeated—for a school committee in Northampton, Massachusetts. As governor of the state in 1919, when it was supposed that he would go no higher, the ordinarily taciturn Coolidge made a statement during the Boston police strike that drew the attention of the country: "There is no right to strike against the public safety by anybody, anywhere, any time."

The people welcomed to the White House this solid, determined man who was of a different breed from the pleasure-loving Harding. "The business of America is business," said Coolidge, and rolled up his sleeves. He did not play golf or cards, ride horseback, swim, hunt, or bowl. His only recreation was walking, and fishing while on vacation. He worked hard and succeeded with his policy of rigid economy in government. Coolidge was the high priest of stability whose main desire was to keep out of trouble.

One reason the Presidency is such a killing job is that in addition to the continual pressure of official business, the Chief Executive is forced to submit to a series of indignities in the form of welcoming groups of various sorts. (Seven presidents have died in office—three from assassins' bullets; several others, broken in health, died soon after leaving the White House.) On these pages are shown some of the ordeals that Coolidge had to endure.

Above: Cal greets Republican leaders of the Sioux Nation.

Left: the unhappy President holds the equally unhappy Louise Sheaffer who has just presented him with a Buddy Poppy on behalf of the Veterans of Foreign Wars.

Above: Coolidge with members of the Jefferson Memorial Foundation. Above, right: opening the baseball season. Right: Cal with the Daughters of the War of 1812. Below: trout fishing (with worms). Below, right: Cal's message refusing a third term.

I do not choose
to run for President
in nineteen twenty
eight

WHEN COOLIDGE WAS PRESIDENT: Nathan Leopold and Richard Loeb (center and right), sons of wealthy Chicago families and postgraduate students at Chicago University, confessed the kidnaping and killing of fourteen-year-old Bobby Franks. The only motive for the crime was the "thrill of it." Ably defended by Clarence Darrow, they were saved from the gallows and got life imprisonment.

Shortly after Coolidge took office, the oil scandals of the previous administration came to light, thus supplying much material for cartoonist Rollin Kirby (below).

"UGH!"

Charles Ponzi, Boston's arch swindler, took in millions with his get-rich-quick scheme in the 1920s, wound up in federal prison.

Increasing auto accidents inspired the invention of a safety bumper (above), which was supposed to grasp a pedestrian and carry him to safety up to a speed of thirty m.p.h.

In July, 1925, John Thomas Scopes, a young biology teacher, was tried for teaching evolution in defiance of Tennessee law. Defended by (above, l. to r.) Clarence Darrow, Arthur Garfield Hayes and Dudley Field Malone, he was found guilty but later freed.

General William Mitchell (standing, center), who was first to sink a ship from a plane, stands trial for insubordination (1925).

The auto came of age in 1925 when traffic lanes were first painted on the Capitol Plaza.

Albert B. Fall (above) was finally brought to book in 1929 when he was sentenced to a year in prison and fined $100,000. Luckier was Harry Daugherty, shown right (in light coat) with his attorney, Max Steuer. He was freed by a hung jury. Fall was the highest government official ever convicted.

While Rudolph Valentino, the screen's first Latin lover, lay in state in Campbell's Funeral Parlor, New York, in 1926 (below), the crowds became so huge and unmanageable that police reserves had to be called out.

Congressman McMillan of South Carolina dances the Charleston on the Capitol grounds.

The Hollywood revolution began in 1927 when Warner Brothers released *The Jazz Singer,* a "talkie" starring Al Jolson, who sang several melodies in blackface (above).

"IF I CATCH YOU INSIDE THE CITY LIMITS I'LL RUN YOU IN"

Chicago's Anglophobe Mayor of the twenties, Big Bill Thompson, said he'd arrest King George if His Majesty ever came to town.

America's hero of the Coolidge era was Colonel Charles A. "Lucky" Lindbergh (right), who flew alone in his monoplane, *Spirit of St. Louis,* from New York to Paris in May, 1927. The nonstop flight of 3,610 miles took 33 hours, 29 minutes, 30 seconds.

HERBERT C. HOOVER 1871–
President 1929–1933

No president ever began an administration under more favorable skies than did Herbert Hoover when he took the oath of office in March, 1929. The country was basking in the sunshine of the "Coolidge Boom" and to its helm came the world's best-known citizen—a humanitarian of international reputation, an efficient engineer with a genius for organization. He also had a genius for making unfortunate utterances. "We in America today are nearer to the final triumph over poverty than ever before in the history of a land," he declared in his acceptance speech, and added that "the poorhouse is vanishing from among us." Everlasting prosperity was the Republican campaign theme—"a chicken in every pot and a car in every garage." When the crash came a few months after Hoover's inauguration, the glittering phrases were derisively quoted from every corner of the land. The hapless President was blamed for the depression although it was worldwide and as unstoppable as a hurricane. He was, in fact, the first president to intervene in a depression. But no man could stem it, though Hoover tried. He summoned to the White House for conferences industrial, commercial, financial and labor leaders and created several fact-finding bodies. He reassured the people that "Prosperity is just around the corner." The depression deepened and Hoover became its symbol. His appearance and actions heightened the impression—the cold, precise personality, the stiff, high collar and round face, his chilly relations with the press.

Hoover was the first president born west of the Mississippi, the first to enter the White House a multimillionaire. He was born in a modest home (above) at West Branch, Iowa, the son of a Quaker blacksmith. The Hoover success story is in keeping with the American tradition of poverty-to-riches by honest toil. Orphaned at nine, he was brought up by relatives in Oregon. At seventeen he entered Stanford University, worked his way through, and upon graduating in 1895 took a job as a common laborer in a Nevada mine. Shortly thereafter the young engineer went to Australia where there was a gold rush, and from there to various parts of the world. By the time he was forty he had a chain of offices encircling the globe and had amassed a fortune as a promoter and financier of mining properties from China, to Russia, Burma and to Africa.

Hoover was unknown outside of mining circles until 1914 when he was appointed head of the American Relief Society in London to help return to the United States many thousands of Americans who had been stranded abroad by the sudden outbreak of World War I. So efficiently did he carry out the job that he was named to organize the feeding of millions of Belgians in their devastated country. When we entered the war President Wilson appointed him United States Food Administrator (left, as he looked in 1917). After the war, as Chief of the Supreme Economic Council of the Allies, Hoover organized great food-relief projects in Europe. Billions of dollars passed through his hands during the seven-year period he was engaged in humanitarian work, but he declined compensation for his services. Back home again, he served as secretary of commerce under Harding and Coolidge.

Below, Hoover is sworn in as president by Chief Justice Taft (appointed by Harding).

Lou Hoover (above) was a fresh-
man, Hoover a senior, when they met
at Stanford University. After their
marriage in 1899 Mrs. Hoover
roamed the world with her husband
for fifteen years. In the White House
the Hoovers entertained lavishly, employed more people than ever before in its history (about 150 all
told, of which some 80 were military aides, police and secret-service
men).

President Hoover once suffered the indignity of being publicly booed at a baseball game and of hearing hundreds chant in unison, "We want beer! We want beer!" as he left the park. There was no doubt about his stand on prohibition. In his acceptance speech for the nomination he said, "I do not favor repeal of the Eighteenth Amendment. I stand for the efficient enforcement of the laws enacted . . . Our country has deliberately undertaken a great social and economic experiment, noble in motive, far-reaching in purpose." The "noble experiment" was investigated by the Wickersham Commission, appointed by Hoover. It found, to no one's surprise, that enforcement had proved wholly inadequate, that the law was distasteful to the American people, that it was freely violated and gave rise to wholesale corruption. Nevertheless, the Commission did not recommend its repeal. This made the unpopular President more unpopular than ever, as the cartoon on this page indicates.

"DON'T MIND ME, GO RIGHT ON WORKING"

In the face of the depression and the repugnant prohibition law, Hoover made a desperate bid for re-election (above). There was little to say. He defended his position of local self-help to the unemployed (rather than federal aid) and warned that if the Democrats got in "the grass will grow in the streets" and "weeds will overrun the fields of millions of farms." He was defeated by a land-slide.

WHEN HOOVER WAS PRESI-DENT: The most momentous crash in Wall Street history took place (October 29, 1929) when over six-teen million shares were traded and averages fell nearly forty points. Above: panic outside the Exchange.

As unemployment rose (to over ten million in 1932) apple vendors appeared on the streets of all major United States cities.

Breadlines and bank failures (above) increased as Hoover's administration came to a close. The production index fell to its lowest point in the country's history and the whole banking structure seemed to be on the verge of utter collapse.

Scarface Al Capone, Chicago overlord of organized crime (below, with a United States Marshal), literally got away with murder for years, but was finally jailed for falsifying his income tax. After serving time at Alcatraz, Al lived royally at his Miami estate.

In July, 1932, a "Bonus Army" of some seven thousand men descended on Washington and refused to leave. On the 28th their shacks were burned on Hoover's orders and the army dispersed.

New York's playboy mayor, Jimmy Walker, is shown here as he took the stand on May 4, 1932, to face Judge Samuel Seabury who was appointed to investigate crime in New York City politics. Jimmy did not do well. As a result of the investigation he was forced to resign, and the following year Fiorello La Guardia was elected on a reform platform. Jimmy went to England.

FRANKLIN DELANO ROOSEVELT 1882–1945
President 1933–1945

Franklin D. Roosevelt, the first President to serve more than two terms and the first to be inaugurated January 20, had much in common with his fifth cousin, Theodore Roosevelt. Both were born to considerable wealth (above, F.D.R.'s birthplace at Hyde Park, New York), both went to Harvard, both began their political careers in the New York legislature, both served as assistant secretaries of the Navy, as governors of New York, and both were nominated vice-president. (T.R. was elected, F.D.R. defeated.) Both became president. Both publicly vowed that they would refuse a third term and both broke their promises. As reformers and leaders of social and economic revolutions (T.R.'s "Square Deal" and F.D.R.'s "New Deal") they were both detested and adored. The parallel continues in their outspoken contempt of what T.R. called the "vested interests," the malefactors of great wealth." This was the group that F.D.R. called "economic royalists," the "money changers" he would drive from the temple.

Today, more than a decade after Franklin Roosevelt's death, the man is still both revered and despised as intensely as if he were living. To attempt to evaluate him here would be presumptuous, for even the most qualified historians cannot agree on his ultimate place in American history.

For instance, Harvard Professor Arthur M. Schlesinger, Jr., a devoted New Dealer and recipient of the Pulitzer Prize for History (1945), rates him as the third greatest president, behind Lincoln and Washington. On the other hand, there are the noted historians Dr. Harry Elmer Barnes and the late Charles A. Beard, to whom Roosevelt was a monumental charlatan.

Roosevelt, say his adherents, was president during the greatest depression and the greatest war in the history of the world, and he defeated them both. To this his critics reply that the depression was deepening in 1937 after four years of Roosevelt (which it was) and that prosperity was restored only because of European war orders. As for the war, while Roosevelt was promising again and again to keep us out of it, he was at the same time deliberately, secretly and unlawfully steering us into it. Furthermore, they say, everything gained in the war was lost at Yalta.

History's final verdict will not be known to this generation.

This photograph taken in June, 1883, shows the future President perched on his father's shoulder. The elder Roosevelt, then fifty-five, married twenty-six-year-old Sara Delan‚ in 1880.

Roosevelt's first inaugural medal (above), designating him as the thirty-first president, was supposed to establish the numerical order of the presidents once and for all. It did not, however. The order was originally upset by the split administrations of Cleveland who became the twenty-second president in 1885 and was followed by Harrison, the twenty-third. Then came Cleveland's second term. To still call him the twenty-second president after the twenty-third had served would lead to confusion, it was thought. So Cleveland was officially designated the twenty-second and the twenty-fourth—still confusing but perhaps less so than the other way. Despite the above medal, F.D.R. is the thirty-second president in practically all biographies, encyclopedias, almanacs and official records.

In the most complete reversal in American history Roosevelt was swept into office by a seven million majority. (Four years before, Hoover's majority had been over six million.) F.D.R. was fifty-one when he took the oath of office, a year younger than Lincoln when he was inaugurated. Like Lincoln, he faced a grave national crisis and immediately went into action. With the authority conferred on him, F.D.R. rushed through a series of measures with dazzling speed: the bank holiday; repeal of prohibition; vast appropriations to be used for relief, for work for the unemployed and to save homes and farms from foreclosure, and business from bankruptcy. "Action and action now" was F.D.R.'s inaugural promise, and action was what the country got.

The above photograph was taken in 1934 when the President and members of his family reviewed the fleet from the U.S.S. *Indianapolis* in New York harbor. Left to right: Eleanor, Mrs. James Roosevelt, F.D.R., James, and the President's mother. The elder Mrs. Roosevelt was the dowager head of Hyde Park where Eleanor and F.D.R. lived for many years. Strong-minded and imperious, she dominated the family home and was adored to an extraordinary degree by her only son.

The famed Roosevelt smile (left) drove some men to fury. Others found it irresistible. To his advocates it reflected Roosevelt's great personal charm. To his critics it characterized his insincerity and deviousness, traits which even his friends admitted he had. His bitter attacks on the well-to-do caused many to wonder how he could fraternize with people like Vincent Astor, on whose luxuriou yacht, *Nourmahal*, the Presiden cruised many times.

Eleanor Roosevelt, the most active and ubiquitous wife of any president, is shown here pursuing some of her typical activities.

Across the top, left to right: speaking before the American Youth Congress in New York; inspecting the basement of a Homestead Home at Des Moines, Iowa; at Lowell Thomas' estate, Pawling, New York. (It is doubtful if Eleanor and Westbrook Pegler, who sits beside her, will ever be this close together again.) Standing are Deems Taylor and the late George Bye, literary agent. Below, left: working in her Val-Kill shop at Hyde Park; below, right: planting a tree in the Memory Garden of the Girl Scouts' "National Little House," Washington.

The tireless mother of five grown children and too many sons-in-law and daughters-in-law (ex and current) to count, Mrs. Roosevelt has traveled some 500,000 miles in the United States alone, has edited a magazine, written a daily and monthly column, given innumerable lectures, laid countless cornerstones, descended a coal mine and has rubbed noses with the New Zealand Maoris.

On December 8, 1941, the day after the attack on Pearl Harbor, the President signed the Declaration War against Japan.

FRANKLIN DELANO ROOSEVELT 1933–1945

The first president to leave the country during a war, Roosevelt conferred with Churchill at Casablanca, Morocco, in January, 1943, to plan military strategy following the North African invasion of the previous fall. It was at this conference that F.D.R. demanded unconditional surrender of the Axis powers. Churchill later stated that "the first time I heard that phrase used it was from the lips of President Roosevelt."

In November, 1943, Roosevelt again left the country for the Cairo and Teheran Conferences. At Teheran, Iran, F.D.R., Churchill and Stalin met together (for the first time) to discuss the invasion of Western Europe. "I believe he (Stalin) is truly representative of the heart and soul of Russia," said Roosevelt after the meeting, "and I believe that we are going to get along very well with him and the Russian people—very well indeed."

On this trip Roosevelt visited Sicily where he met General Eisenhower (below) on December 8, just two years to the day after the signing of the Declaration of War against Japan. By that time Italy had surrendered to the Allies and was at war with Germany.

WHEN ROOSEVELT WAS PRESIDENT: "Public Enemy Number One," John Dillinger, America's most notorious bandit, was considered a hero by some, as this billboard near Loretto, Pennsylvania, indicates. He was killed by the FBI in 1934.

A powerful weapon used by labor with great frequency in the '30s was the illegal sit-down strike. Below: workers take possession of the Fisher Body Plant, St. Louis, 1937.

Senator Huey (Kingfish) Long promised every family a five-thousand-dollar annual income, to be paid for by the rich.

The country was shocked in 1937 when F.D.R. tried (and failed) to "pack the Supreme Court" (above), *i.e.*, swell its numbers with members sympathetic to the New Deal.

At a cost of $150,000,000, New York's World Fair opened in April, 1939, ran until October, 1940. Over sixty countries were represented.

Defiant to the last, Sewell Avery (left), head of Montgomery Ward Company, was carried from his office by United States soldiers when he refused to leave the strike-bound plant.

The sixty-million-dollar French liner *Normandie* burned and capsized at her pier in New York, February 9, 1942. Beyond salvage, she was scrapped.

Roosevelt was a sick man when he met Churchill and Stalin at Yalta, in the Crimean Peninsula, in February, 1945 (above). Uncle Joe—as F.D.R. often called the Russian dictator in his official communiqués to Churchill—proved to be a shrewd bargainer at the conference. In return for his promise to fight Japan, Stalin was granted extraordinary rights in Asia and Eastern Europe, even though Roosevelt knew at the time that the atomic bomb would soon be tested. (As it turned out Russia did not enter the Japanese war until after the first atomic bomb had been dropped. She was at war with Japan for only six days. Later Stalin violated every Yalta agreement which guaranteed free elections in Europe.)

The secret agreements reached by the three leaders caused the man in the street to wonder about the decisions made at Yalta (note cartoon left). So secret were they that even James F. Byrnes, a Roosevelt adviser at the conference, was kept in the dark.

WHAT DECISIONS?

The Franklin D. Roosevelt Library at Hyde Park on land donated to the government by F.D.R. during his lifetime. The building was raised by voluntary subscription (some 400,000) and is administered by the National Archives. Over half a million people annually pay twenty-five cents each to visit the library-museum which contains thousands of books, photographs, movie films and museum objects. At the main entrance (above) is a bust of the President which was presented by the International Ladies' Garment Workers' Union. In a rose garden nearby a plain white marble tombstone marks the grave of the thirty-second President.

HARRY S. TRUMAN 1884–
President 1945–1953

On April 12, 1945, less than three months after his inauguration to the Vice-Presidency, Harry Truman was summoned to the White House to receive the yet unreleased news that Roosevelt had died that afternoon at Warm Springs, Georgia, of a cerebral hemorrhage. That evening shortly after seven o'clock in the presence of his family (above, Mrs. Truman and daughter Margaret) and government officials, he was sworn in by Chief Justice Harlan Fiske Stone. Thus did Truman become the seventh accidental president. It was a dazed and humble President who said to friendly reporters the next day, "I've got the most awful responsibility a man ever had. If you fellows ever pray, pray for me." The fact that Truman carried out his responsibilities with courage and went on to win the Presidency virtually by himself was a wonder to many, considering his background.

A Missouri farmer with a high-school education, Truman did not leave the family farm until he was thirty-three, when he joined the army and went off to war in 1917. Two years later he returned with the rank of captain, and opened a haberdashery shop in Kansas City, which soon failed. Broke and without much future, Truman was picked up by Tom Pendergast, Kansas City's crooked political boss, who put him on his slate. Truman made a creditable record in local politics, kept his hands clean and was eventually awarded a United States senatorship by the Boss. In the Senate he had an undistinguished career until he formed the Truman War Investigating Committee, which acted as a watchdog on government wartime expenditures. Its success brought his name to the foreground. In 1944, on the eve of the Democratic convention, Roosevelt decided to discard Henry Wallace, then vice-president, and suggested as a replacement either William O. Douglas or Truman, provided that the names were approved by Sidney Hillman, C.I.O. labor boss. Hence the phrase, "clear it with Sidney." Sidney thought Harry would be fine.

Gay Harry posed for this picture (left) with Lauren Bacall, "The Look," at the National Press Club Canteen in Washington in 1945, a year that was crowded with the most climactic events in our history: the battles of the Bulge and Iwo Jima, the Yalta and Potsdam Conferences, the first atomic bomb, the surrender of Germany and Japan, the deaths of Roosevelt, Mussolini and Hitler, and the United States acceptance of the United Nations Charter.

The presidential yacht, the U.S.S. *Williamsburg,* provided Truman and his friends many weekends of relaxation on the Potomac. It is shown below steaming into the harbor at St. Thomas, Virgin Islands, with the President and his party aboard.

Truman's frugal mode of living on his modest salary as senator—a salary augmented by that of his wife who served as his secretary—underwent a considerable change when he became president. In addition to the *Williamsburg,* he inherited from Roosevelt the *Sacred Cow* (above, with seven-man crew), a four-motored Douglas C-54 Skymaster equipped with a special elevator and de luxe interior.

Below right, the electronic control board in the $119,000 railroad communication car used by Truman. Its radiotelephone, teletype, and code transmitters enabled the President to communicate instantly with the White House, ships at sea, military installations or any foreign capital. Below left, on his special compaign train Truman receives an ear of corn from an Iowa youngster.

Truman's salary was raised by Congress from $75,000 to $100,000 a year and the expense account of the office from $40,000 to $90,000 (tax free).

AT BASEMENT LEVEL

In the "Give 'em Hell" campaign of 1948 (above), the sixty-four-year-old Truman traveled 31,000 miles and made over 350 speeches, hammering away at every whistle stop at the Republican "do nothing" Eightieth Congress. Almost no one thought he could win, not even his supporters, and least of all the Republicans who were lulled to sleep by the results of the public-opinion polls. Everything indicated a walkover for his opponent, Governor Thomas E. Dewey of New York. But Dewey, cold and colorless, refused to roll up his sleeves and resorted to dignified platitudes. The result was the biggest upset in the history of presidential elections. The *Chicago Daily Tribune* was so confident of a Dewey victory that it announced his election before the final returns came in, much to Truman's glee.

The agreement made at Potsdam designating the thirty-eighth parallel as the dividing line between Soviet and American troops in Korea was broken when the North Korean Army crossed the line on June 25, 1950. Truman acted instantly. That same day he ordered General Douglas MacArthur to go to the aid of South Korea, and the war was on.

In October Truman flew to Wake Island to confer with MacArthur (above), then the United Nations commander in chief. MacArthur returned to Korea and opened a major offensive, but was prevented from following his advantage on orders from Washington. Truman dismissed him from his Korean and Japanese posts in 1951.

WHEN TRUMAN WAS PRESI-
DENT: The atomic age began with
the destruction of the Japanese city
of Hiroshima on August 6, 1945,
when 78,000 noncombatants were
killed with one blast (left). The bil-
lowing smoke rose twenty thousand
feet above the city and spread over
ten thousand feet at the base of the
rising column. Three days later a
second A-bomb was dropped on
Nagasaki, killing 74,000.

Aboard the U.S.S. *Missouri* in
Tokyo Bay on September 2, 1945,
MacArthur watched General Umezu
of Japan sign the Articles of Surrender.

New York's heaviest snowfall
(25.8 inches) crippled the city, December 26, 1947, and brought all surface transportation to a standstill.

A five-man crime committee headed by Senator Estes Kefauver toured the country in 1951, investigating illegal operations of politicians, police, racketeers and gamblers in several cities. Among the five hundred witnesses interviewed was New York's underworld boss Frank Costello (above) who was later sent to jail. Kefauver's committee reported that gambling involved over twenty million dollars annually.

Alger Hiss (left) was sentenced to five years in jail in 1951 following his conviction of perjury in connection with the turning over of government secrets to the Soviets.

The American superliner *United States* broke the Atlantic record in 1952 by crossing to England in three days, ten hours, forty minutes.

The new White House (above) is not unlike the building of 1825 (left) in outward appearance, despite the addition of the ten-thousand-dollar balcony installed by Truman. (These pictures show the south front, the earlier one being a view from Tibre Creek, since filled in to make Constitution Avenue.) Late in 1948, when it was discovered that the White House was in danger of complete collapse, the Trumans moved to nearby Blair House, where they stayed until the old building was strengthened and restored at a cost of $5,761,000. In March, 1952, the Trumans returned to a completely modernized White House with air conditioning and running ice water in every room. Counting storage and utility rooms, the building contains 132 rooms, twenty baths and showers and twenty-nine fireplaces. There are fifty-four rooms and sixteen baths in the part of the house used as living quarters.

Above: Lincoln's bedroom, which is used for high-ranking male guests. The long bed, covered by a spread crocheted by Mrs. Calvin Coolidge, was made especially for Lincoln.

The grandest and largest room in the White House is the East Room (above) which is used for State functions, Christmas parties, balls and musicales. It is seventy-nine feet long, thirty-six and three-quarters feet wide with a twenty-two-foot-high ceiling, and has four fireplaces and three huge gold-plated and crystal chandeliers. In this room Abigail Adams, the first mistress of the White House, hung out her wash. Lincoln's soldiers were quartered here while the Confederates threatened Washington. In it Nellie Grant and Alice Roosevelt (T.R.'s daughter) were married, and funeral services were held for William Henry Harrison, Taylor, Lincoln, Harding and Franklin Roosevelt. On its walls, fitted into panels, are the portraits of George Washington (the one Dolly Madison saved) and Martha Washington. The grand piano, a gift from Steinway and Sons, has ornate gold eagles for legs and gilded scenes on its sides of American folk dancing.

Below: the all-electric modern kitchen equipped with stainless-steel utensils and opaque glass walls. Located on the ground floor, the room has dumb-waiters to transfer food to a pantry which connects with state and family dining rooms on the main floor.

DWIGHT D. EISENHOWER 1890–
President 1953–

Dwight David Eisenhower, America's hero of World War II, is the third regular army man to become president, the first to be born in Texas and the first of German ancestry. Over half of our presidents (nineteen) have served their country in uniform, beginning with Washington, but all save three were citizen-soldiers. The three exceptions are Zachary Taylor, U. S. Grant and

Eisenhower—dedicated Army men with no political experience when the Presidency called.

Eisenhower was born in Denison, Texas, on October 14, 1890, the third of seven sons (one died in infancy) of David and Ida Stover Eisenhower. Texas was the future President's birthplace by accident, for his parents came there from Kansas, stayed less than two years and then returned to Abilene when he was five months old. All the other Eisenhower boys were born in Kansas and all grew up in Abilene where their father earned a meager salary as a mechanic in a creamery. (He had previously failed in business in Kansas, and during the Texas interlude had worked in a railroad machine shop.)

The above picture of the Eisenhower family was taken when Dwight (extreme left) was eight years old. A quarter of a century later at a family reunion in Abilene the same group again posed for a picture, in the identical position they appear in above. At that time the Eisenhower boys were on their way to success. From them were to come a president, an engineer, a banker, a lawyer, a businessman and a college president—a remarkable record in view of their poor circumstances in the early days. The Eisenhower parents, members of the Church of the Brethren in Christ, reared their sons in a strict religious environment.

In high school Ike—as he was then called—played football and baseball, and after graduating worked around town for over a year. In 1910 he took a War Department competitive examination for appointment to the service schools. A candidate could then apply for either Annapolis or West Point, or he could list himself as an "either," *i.e.,* no preference. Although Ike had his heart set on Annapolis, he put down "either" on his application in the belief that by so doing his chances of success would be increased. A few months later the twenty-year-old Ike found himself climbing the hill to the Point.

The picture on the opposite page shows Cadet Eisenhower in his second year at West Point (1912) as the halfback understudy of Geoffrey Keyes, the Army's star of the previous year. Ike played in six games and showed great promise as a hard-tackling, hard-running back. His biggest thrill was downing Jim Thorpe in the Carlisle game. A broken knee finished his football career.

In 1915 Ike graduated from West Point (slightly above average in scholarship; in conduct 95th in a class of 164) and was sent to Fort Houston in San Antonio. There he met Mamie Geneva Doud, the daughter of a Denver businessman. They were married in Denver on July 1, 1916 (above). Ike refused to sit down until after the ceremony for fear of spoiling the knife-like crease in his trousers.

Promotions were slow during the first twenty-five years of Ike's moderately distinguished army career. Although he rose to the rank of lieutenant colonel (temporary) in the first World War, he dropped back to captain in 1920, then up to major the same year and for the next sixteen years did not budge. The future did not seem promising—perhaps a colonelcy some day. He had been forced to spend World War I in this country and now, in 1936 at the age of forty-six, he was still a major. But things happened rapidly after that. From lieutenant colonel in March, 1941, Ike rose to the rank of full general in twenty-three months.

A few days after Pearl Harbor Eisenhower was summoned to Washington by Chief of Staff George C. Marshall, and put to a test on the problem of Pacific strategy. How many other officers had been given that same assignment is not known, but it is known that Eisenhower's brilliant design stood out above all the others. He was subsequently made Chief of the War Plans Division and was sent to England to prepare a plan on American participation in Europe. Again Ike scored with a masterful directive. This led to his command of the European Theater and later to his appointment by Roosevelt as Supreme Commander for the invasion of Europe. Eisenhower's magnificent achievement in this role was due not only to his strategic planning but also to his consummate tact, his engaging personality and his ability to be tough and forceful at the right time.

A man with such qualities ought to make a good president, many people thought in the summer of 1947 when a boom was set off upon his announcement that he was leaving the army to become president of Columbia University. He was so popular that he probably could have had the nomination of either party for the asking, but Ike said no in terms that could not be mistaken. By 1952, however, there was such a demand for him to run that he could no longer refuse. While still in Europe on active service again he permitted his name to be used in the Republican ballot in some states where the delegates were chosen by ballot.

Below, Ike returns in glory to Abilene just before his campaign for the nomination. After a bitter contest between Taft and Eisenhower supporters over delegates, Ike was nominated on the first ballot.

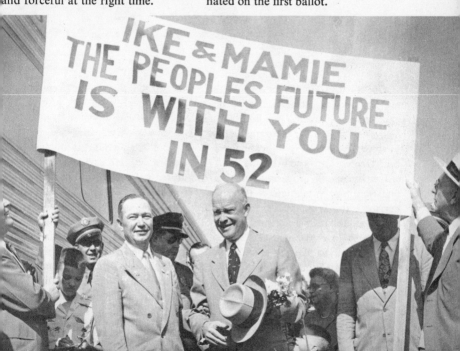

Governor Adlai Stevenson of Illinois made witty campaign speeches and was an appealing candidate, but he was no match for the popular Ike. Moreover, he was handicapped by the Democratic record: the indecisive Korean War, Communist infiltration in Washington ("a red herring" to Truman), the inflated "Truman dollar," and crime and corruption in government. Even Stevenson referred to the state of affairs as the "mess in Washington." The Democrats were put on the defensive. They praised the F.D.R. record and warned that if the Republicans got in, a depression was sure to follow. Organized labor, the tail of the Democratic kite, endorsed Stevenson, but to no avail. Eisenhower won hands down. He polled nearly seven million more votes than Stevenson (442 electoral votes to 89) and broke the solid South by taking Virginia, Florida, Tennessee and Texas.

Above, President Truman and his wife greet the Eisenhowers at the White House, January 20, 1953, just before the President-elect left for the Capitol and the swearing-in ceremonies.

The petite and gracious Mamie Doud Eisenhower has her husband's gift for getting along with people, and is one of the more popular of the White House hostesses. She willingly performs the duties of a First Lady, but consistently avoids the spotlight and does not interfere with the business of government. Army assignments kept the Eisenhowers so much on the move that they had no permanent home until 1952 when the President bought a farm near Gettysburg.

Mamie's inaugural dress, which she wears in the above portrait, will be added to the Smithsonian Institution's collection of dresses of the First Ladies when her White House regime is over.

DURING EISENHOWER'S ADMINISTRATION: The White House was picketed for twelve days by sympathizers of Julius and Ethel Rosenberg, convicted atom spies. The couple died in the electric chair at Sing Sing on June 19, 1953.

The three-year inconclusive Korean War came to an end in July, 1953, with the signing of the Armistice at Panmunjom. United States casualties: 33,237 dead; 103,376 wounded.

FBI Chief Edgar Hoover (above) testified that he had informed President Truman on three occasions that government official Harry Dexter White was a member of a Communist spy ring. The result of Hoover's report: White was promoted.

5 CONGRESSMEN SHOT BY 3 GALLERY GUNMEN

Headlines like this spread across the newspapers of the country on March 1, 1954, when Puerto Rican extremists blazed away with automatic pistols from the House gallery and wounded five Congressmen.

The President's favorite cartoon of himself (below) appeared in the Washington *Star*. It shows Ike with his signals crossed, about to drive a baseball from the White House lawn as Clark Griffith, owner of the Washington Senators, rushes to halt him.

Controversy between Senator Joseph R. McCarthy and Army Secretary Robert T. Stevens over the promotion of an officer suspected of being a Communist led to the 36-day-long Army-McCarthy hearings in 1954. (Above, McCarthy and counsel Roy M. Cohn.) Later, McCarthy was condemned by the Senate for undignified conduct.

The most sports-minded president since Teddy Roosevelt, Eisenhower is an accomplished dry-fly fisherman, a fine shot with both pistol and shotgun, and a better than fair golfer. Like many an ex-athlete, Ike gets relaxation out of competitive sports, especially golf—by far his favorite game—which he plays hard and to win. The stakes are nominal, usually a dollar Nassau. (Above left, he goes around with Vice-President Nixon at the Cherry Hills Country Club, Denver, Colorado.) Ike once said that the C.I.O. kept tabs on the number of his golf outings.

Like Churchill, Ike is an amateur painter. In his studio in the White House he works with great concentration on his landscapes and while he is painting (the periods last anywhere from fifteen minutes to two hours) he will not talk to anyone. After golf and painting, his favorite relaxations are, in order: playing with his three grandchildren, bridge, TV, movies, reading (mostly Westerns), cooking (he never washes the dishes), fishing and shooting.

The first presidential news conference covered by movie and TV cameras took place on January 19, 1955 (above), and was soon beamed to the nation's living rooms. The country saw the President answer a reporter's request for an "appraisal of your first two years." In his reply Eisenhower listed the end of the Korean War, and a more stable foreign situation in general. At home, taxes and spending had been cut, said the President, and the economy is sound and prosperous.

"Dynamic conservatism" is the apt phrase the President uses to define his administration. He said: "I believe we should be conservative. I believe we should conserve everything that is basic to our system. We should

be dynamic in applying it to the problems of the day so that all 163 million Americans will profit from it."

'NEW ROLE'

Chronology of the Presidents

GEORGE WASHINGTON

THOMAS JEFFERSON

1732 Born Westmoreland County, Virginia, February 22
1748 Began surveying in the West
1749 Official surveyor of Culpeper County
1752 Adjutant General of Virginia Militia
1753 Sent to Pennsylvania to warn French out of Ohio Valley
1754 Surrendered Fort Necessity to French
1755 Aide to General Braddock; Commander in Chief of the Virginia Forces
1759 Married Martha Dandridge Custis
1759-74 Member House of Burgesses
1774-75 Member Continental Congress
1775-83 General and Commander in Chief of the Continental Forces
1787-88 Chairman Constitutional Convention
1789-97 President
1799 Died at Mount Vernon, December 14

1743 Born Shadwell, Virginia, April 13
1762 Graduated William and Mary College
1767 Admitted to the Bar
1772 Married Martha Wayles Skelton
1769-74 Member House of Burgesses
1775-76 Member Continental Congress
1776-79 Member Virginia House of Delegates
1779-81 Governor of Virginia
1783-85 Member Continental Congress
1785-89 Minister to France
1790-93 Secretary of State
1797-1801 Vice-President
1801-09 President
1826 Died July 4

JOHN ADAMS

JAMES MADISON

1735 Born Braintree (Quincy), Mass., Oct. 30
1755 Graduated from Harvard
1758 Admitted to the Bar
1764 Married Abigail Smith
1774 Elected to Continental Congress
1778 Commissioner to France
1785 Minister to England
1789-97 Vice-President
1797-1801 President
1826 Died July 4

1751 Born Port Conway, Virginia, March 16
1771 Graduated from Princeton
1780-83 Member Continental Congress
1787 Member Constitutional Convention
1789-97 Member United States Congress
1794 Married Dolly Payne Todd
1801-09 Secretary of State
1809-17 President
1826-36 Rector, University of Virginia
1836 Died June 28

JAMES MONROE

1758 Born Westmoreland Cty., Va., April 28
1776 Graduated William and Mary College
1776 Enlisted in Continental Army
1786 Married Eliza Kortright
1786–90 Practiced law, Fredericksburg, Va.
1790–94 United States Senator
1794–96 Minister to France
1799–1802 Governor of Virginia
1803–07 Minister to England
1811 Governor of Virginia
1811–17 Secretary of State
(1814–15 Secretary of War)
1817–25 President
1831 Died July 4

ANDREW JACKSON

1767 Born Waxhaw, S.C., March 15
1780–81 Served as messenger in Revolution
1787 Admitted to the Bar
1788 Went to Nashville, Tenn., practiced law
1791 Married Rachel Donelson Robards (remarried in 1794)
1796–97 Member of Congress
1797–98 United States Senator
1798–1804 Justice of Tenn. Supreme Court
1802 Major General of Tennessee Militia
1812–15 Served in War of 1812
1817–18 Commanded troops, Seminole War
1821 Governor of Florida Territory
1823–25 United States Senator
1829–37 President
1845 Died June 8

JOHN QUINCY ADAMS

1767 Born Braintree (Quincy), Massachusetts, July 11
1781 Secretary to United States Minister to Russia
1788 Graduated from Harvard
1791 Admitted to the Bar
1794 Minister to Holland
1797 Married Louisa Catherine Johnson
1797–1801 Minister to Berlin
1803–08 United States Senator
1809–11 Minister to Russia
1814 Peace Commissioner at Ghent
1815–17 Minister to England
1817–25 Secretary of State
1825–29 President
1831–48 Member of Congress
1848 Died February 23

MARTIN VAN BUREN

1782 Born Kinderhook, N.Y., Dec. 5
1803 Admitted to the Bar
1807 Married Hannah Hoes
1813–15 New York State Senator
1815–19 Attorney General of New York
1821–29 United States Senator
1829 Governor of New York
1829–31 Secretary of State
1831–32 Minister to England
1833–37 Vice-President
1837–41 President
1840 Unsuccessful Democratic candidate for President
1848 Again defeated for President as Free-Soil candidate
1862 Died July 24

WILLIAM HENRY HARRISON

JAMES K. POLK

1773 Born Berkeley, Virginia, February 9
1791–96 Active in Indian fighting in the Northwest
1795 Married to Anna Symmes
1798 Secretary, Northwest Territory
1799–1801 Territorial Delegate to Congress
1801–13 Governor of Indiana Territory
1811–12 Led United States troops against Indians in Northwest
1812–14 Major General in War of 1812
1816–19 Member of Congress from Ohio
1825–28 United States Senator
1828–29 Minister to Colombia
1836 Unsuccessful Whig candidate for President
1841 President
1841 Died April 4

1795 Born Mecklenburg County, North Carolina, November 2
1806 Moved to Tennessee
1818 Graduated from University of North Carolina
1820 Admitted to the Bar
1823–25 Member Tennessee Legislature
1824 Married Sarah Childress
1825–39 Member of Congress
1939–41 Governor of Tennessee
1841 Defeated for Governor
1843 Again defeated for Governor
1845–49 President
1849 Died June 15

JOHN TYLER

ZACHARY TAYLOR

1790 Born Greenway, Virginia, March 29
1807 Graduated William and Mary College
1809 Admitted to the Bar
1813 Married Letitia Christian (died 1842)
1816–21 Member of Congress
1823–25 Member of Virginia Legislature
1825–26 Governor of Virginia
1827–36 United States Senator
1841 Vice-President, March 4–April 4
1841–45 President
1844 Married Julia Gardiner
1861–62 Member of Confederate Congress
1862 Died January 18

1784 Born Orange County, Virginia, November 24
1785 Moved with family to Kentucky
1808 Commissioned Lieutenant, United States Army
1810 Married Margaret Smith Promoted to Captain
1812–15 Served in War of 1812
1816–32 Assigned to various Army posts
1832 Colonel in Black Hawk War
1836–37 Brigadier General in Seminole War
1845–47 Engaged in Mexican War
1849–50 President
1850 Died July 9

MILLARD FILLMORE

1800 Born Locke, New York, January 7
1823 Admitted to the Bar
1826 Married Abigail Powers (died 1853)
1828–31 Member of New York Assembly
1833–35 Member of Congress
1837–45 Member of Congress
1844 Defeated for Governor of New York
1846–47 Chancellor University of Buffalo
1847 Comptroller of New York State
1849–50 Vice-President
1850–53 President
1856 Defeated for President
1858 Married Caroline McIntosh
1862 President Buffalo Historical Society
1874 Died March 8

JAMES BUCHANAN

1791 Born near Mercersburg, Pa., April 23
1809 Graduated from Dickinson College
1812 Admitted to the Bar
1814 Served in War of 1812
1815–16 Member Pennsylvania Legislature
1821–31 Member of Congress
1832–34 Minister to Russia
1834–45 United States Senator
1845–49 Secretary of State
1853–56 Minister to Great Britain
1857–61 President
1868 Died June 1

FRANKLIN PIERCE

1804 Born Hillsboro, New Hampshire, November 23
1824 Graduated from Bowdoin College
1827 Admitted to the Bar
1829–33 Member New Hampshire Legislature
1833–37 Member of Congress
1834 Married Jane Means Appleton
1837–42 United States Senator
846–48 Served in Mexican War
853–57 President
869 Died October 8

ABRAHAM LINCOLN

1809 Born near Hodgenville, Kentucky, February 12
1816 Moved with parents to Indiana
1828 Made first flatboat trip to New Orleans (second in 1831)
1831–37 Settled in New Salem, Illinois: Captain in Black Hawk War, store owner, surveyor, postmaster
1834–42 Member Illinois Legislature
1836 Admitted to the Bar
1837 Moved to Springfield, Illinois, practiced law
1842 Married Mary Todd
1847-49 Member of Congress
1858 Defeated for United States Senate
1861–65 President
1865 Died April 15

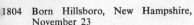

**ANDREW
JOHNSON**

**RUTHERFORD
B. HAYES**

1808	Born Raleigh, N.C., Dec. 29
1826	Opened a tailor shop in Greenville, Tennessee
1827	Married Eliza McCardle
1830–33	Mayor of Greenville
1835–43	State Representative and Senator
1843–53	Member of Congress
1853–57	Governor of Tennessee
1857–62	United States Senator
1862–65	Military Governor of Tennessee
1865	Vice-President, March 4–April 15
1865–69	President
1875	United States Senator
	Died July 31

1822	Born Delaware, Ohio, October 4
1842	Graduated from Kenyon College, Ohio
1845	Graduated from Harvard Law School
	Admitted to the Bar
1852	Married Lucy Webb
1858–60	City Solicitor of Cincinnati
1861–65	Served in the Civil War
1865–67	Member of Congress
1868–72	Governor of Ohio
1872	Defeated for Congress
1876–77	Governor of Ohio
1877–81	President
1881	Retired to Fremont, Ohio
1893	Died January 17

ULYSSES S. GRANT

**JAMES
A. GARFIELD**

1822	Born Point Pleasant, Ohio, April 27
1843	Graduated from West Point
1846–48	Served in Mexican War
1848	Married Julia Dent
1854	Resigned from the Army
1854–61	Farmer, real estate dealer, clerk in Missouri and Ohio
1861–65	Engaged in the Civil War
1866	Promoted to rank of General
1869–77	President
1880	Formed stock brokerage firm, New York
1884	Failed in business
1885	Wrote memoirs
	Died July 23

1831	Born Orange, Ohio, November 19
1856	Graduated from Williams College
1857–61	Instructor at, and President of Hiram Institute, Ohio
1858	Married Lucretia Rudolph
1859–61	State Senator
1860	Admitted to the Bar
1861–63	Served in the Civil War
1863–80	Member of Congress
1880	Elected United States Senator
1881	President
	Died September 19

CHESTER A. ARTHUR

BENJAMIN HARRISON

1830 Born Fairfield, Vermont, October 5
1848 Graduated from Union College
1851–53 Taught school at Pownall, Vt.
1853 Admitted to the Bar, New York City
1859 Married Ellen Lewis Herndon
1861–62 Quartermaster General of N. Y. State
1871–78 Collector of the Port of New York
1878–81 Practiced law in New York
1881 Vice-President, March 4–Sept. 19
1881–85 President
1886 Died November 18

1833 Born North Bend, Ohio, August 20
1852 Graduated Miami University, Ohio
1853 Married Caroline Scott (died 1892) Admitted to the Bar
1854 Practiced law in Indianapolis
1857–61 City Attorney
1861–62 Reporter, Indiana Supreme Court
1862–65 Served in the Civil War
1876 Defeated for Governor of Indiana
1881–87 United States Senator
1889–93 President
1896 Married Mary Scott Lord Dimmick
1901 Died March 13

GROVER CLEVELAND

WILLIAM McKINLEY

837 Born Caldwell, New Jersey, March 18
841 Moved with parents to New York State
859 Admitted to the Bar at Buffalo
863–65 Assistant District Attorney of Erie County, New York
870–73 Sheriff of Erie County
882 Mayor of Buffalo
883–85 Governor of New York
885–89 President
886 Married Frances Folsom
888 Defeated for re-election
889–93 Practiced law in New York City
893–97 President
08 Died June 24

1843 Born Niles, Ohio, January 29
1860 Attended Allegheny College, Pennsylvania
1861–65 Served in Civil War
1867–77 Practiced law, Canton, Ohio
1871 Married Ida Saxton
1877–91 Member of Congress (except for 1883–85)
1892–96 Governor of Ohio
1897–1901 President
1901 Died September 14

THEODORE ROOSEVELT

1858 Born New York, N.Y., October 27
1880 Graduated from Harvard
1880 Married Alice H. Lee (died 1884)
1882–84 Member of New York Assembly
1884–86 Operated ranches, North Dakota
1886 Married Edith Kermit Carow
1889–95 Member of United States Civil Service Commission
1895–97 President, N. Y. City Police Board
1897–98 Assistant Secretary of Navy
1898 Colonel of Rough Riders
1898–1900 Governor of New York
1901 Vice-President, March 4–Sept. 14
1901–09 President
1909–10 Hunted big game in Africa
1912 Defeated for President
1913–14 Explored Brazilian jungles
1919 Died January 6

WOODROW WILSON

1856 Born Staunton, Virginia, December 28
1873–74 Attended Davidson College, N.C.
1879 Graduated from Princeton
1882 Graduated from University of Virginia Law School Admitted to the Bar
1882–83 Practiced law at Atlanta, Georgia
1883–85 Graduate student at Johns Hopkins
1885 Married Ellen Axson (died 1914)
1885–88 Instructor in history, Bryn Mawr
1888–90 Professor at Wesleyan University
1890–1902 Professor at Princeton
1902–10 President of Princeton
1911–13 Governor of New Jersey
1913–21 President
1915 Married Edith Bolling Galt
1924 Died February 3

WILLIAM HOWARD TAFT

1857 Born Cincinnati, Ohio, September 15
1878 Graduated from Yale
1880 Admitted to the Bar
1886 Married Helen Herron
1887–90 Judge, Ohio Superior Court
1890–92 United States Solicitor General
1892–1900 U. S. Circuit Court Judge
1900–04 Commissioner and Governor of the Philippines
1904–08 Secretary of War
1909–13 President
1913–21 Professor of Law at Yale
1921–30 Chief Justice, U. S. Supreme Court
1930 Died March 8

WARREN G. HARDING

1865 Born Corsica, Ohio, November 2
1879–82 Attended Ohio Central College
1884 Became editor of the Marion *Star*
1891 Married Florence De Wolfe Kling
1900–04 Member Ohio State Senate
1904–06 Lieutenant Governor of Ohio
1910 Defeated for Governor
1915–21 United States Senator
1921–23 President
1923 Died August 2

CALVIN COOLIDGE

1872 Born Plymouth, Vermont, July 4
1895 Graduated from Amherst College
1897 Admitted to the Massachusetts Bar
1899 City Councilman, Northampton, Massachusetts
1900–01 City Solicitor
1904 Clerk of the courts
1905 Married Grace Anne Goodhue
1907–08 Member, state legislature
1910–11 Mayor of Northampton
1912–15 Member, state senate
1916–18 Lieutenant Governor
1919–20 Governor
1921–23 Vice-President
1923–29 President
1933 Died January 5

FRANKLIN DELANO ROOSEVELT

1882 Born Hyde Park, N.Y., January 30
1904 Graduated from Harvard
1905 Married Eleanor Roosevelt
1907 Graduated from Columbia Law School
Admitted to New York Bar
1907–10 Practiced law in New York City
1911–13 Member, state senate
1913–20 Assistant Secretary of the Navy
1920 Defeated for Vice-President
1921 Stricken with infantile paralysis
1921–29 Practiced law in New York City
1929–33 Governor of New York
1933–45 President
1945 Died April 12

HERBERT C. HOOVER

1874 Born West Branch, Iowa, August 10
1895 Graduated from Stanford University
1895–1914 Mining engineer
1899 Married Lou Henry
1914–15 Chairman of the American Relief Committee, London
1915–19 Commissioner for Belgian Relief
1917–19 United States Food Administrator
1919–21 Served on various government economic and food councils including the American Relief Administration
1921–28 Secretary of Commerce
1929–33 President
1933 Appointed to various welfare and economic commissions

HARRY S. TRUMAN

1884 Born Lamar, Missouri, May 8
1901–06 In Kansas City employed as reporter on the *Star,* railroad timekeeper, bank clerk
1906–17 Operated family farm
1917–19 Served in World War I
1919 Married Elizabeth Virginia Wallace
1919–22 Operated a haberdashery store in Kansas City
1922–24 Judge, Jackson County Court
1925–26 Automobile salesman, manager of a building and loan company
1926–34 Presiding Judge, Jackson County
1935–45 United States Senator
1945 Vice-President, January 20–April 12
1945–53 President

DWIGHT D. EISENHOWER

1890 Born Denison, Texas, October 14
1891 Moved with family to Abilene, Kansas
1915 Graduated from West Point
1916 Married Mamie Geneva Doud
1916–41 Assigned to various military

posts, advanced through grades from lieutenant to colonel
1941 Made Brigadier General
1942 Lieutenant General, Allied Commander in Chief of North Africa
1943 Commanding General of Allied Powers in European Theater
1944 Invaded Normandy, General of the Army
1945–48 Chief of Staff, United States Army
1948–52 President of Columbia University
1950–52 Supreme Commander of Allied Powers in Europe
1952 Resigned from the Army
1953 Inaugurated President

Facts About the Presidents

All thirty-three men who served as president have been American-born. Those born before the United States became independent in 1776 were Washington, Adams, Jefferson, Madison, Monroe, John Quincy Adams, Jackson and William Henry Harrison. Van Buren was the first president born under the American flag.

Only three presidents were born west of the Mississippi. They were Hoover (Iowa), Truman (Missouri), and Eisenhower (Texas). Eight presidents were born in Virginia, seven in Ohio.

Average age upon first taking office —fifty-four; at death—sixty-seven. W. H. Harrison at sixty-eight was the oldest president; Theodore Roosevelt at forty-two, the youngest.

Lincoln was the tallest president—six feet, four inches; Taft, who weighed three hundred pounds plus, the largest; Madison—five feet, four inches, the smallest.

Seven presidents died in office—W. H. Harrison, Taylor, Lincoln, Garfield, McKinley, Harding and F. D. Roose-

velt. Lincoln, Garfield and McKinley were assassinated.

Jackson was the first president to travel by train; T. Roosevelt, the first to fly; F. D. Roosevelt, the first to fly while president; Eisenhower, the first and only president to hold a pilot's license.

Taft was the first president of the Union of the forty-eight states.

The twice-married presidents were Tyler, Fillmore, B. Harrison, T. Roosevelt and Wilson; Tyler had the most children—fourteen, seven by each of his two wives; Buchanan was the only president who never married.

Two presidents served in Congress after their terms of office—John Quincy Adams in the House of Representatives, Andrew Johnson in the Senate.

F. D. Roosevelt had the longest administration—twelve years, one month and eight days; William Henry Harrison, the shortest—one month.

Harding was the first president to speak over the radio, Coolidge the first to broadcast an inaugural address, and Eisenhower's inauguration the first to be telecast.

Presidential Elections 1789–1952

(F) Federalist; (D) Democrat; (R) Republican; (DR) Democrat-Republican; (NR) National Republican; (W) Whig; (P) People's; (Pr) Progressive; (SR) State's Rights

YEAR	PRESIDENTS ELECTED	POPULAR VOTE	ELECTORAL VOTE	DEFEATED CANDIDATES	POPULAR VOTE	ELECTORAL VOTE
1789	George Washington (No party)	Unknown	69	No opponent		
1792	George Washington (F)	Unknown	132	No opponent		
1796	John Adams (F)	Unknown	71	Thomas Jefferson (DR)		68
1800	Thomas Jefferson (DR)	Unknown	73	Aaron Burr (DR)		73
1804	Thomas Jefferson (DR)	Unknown	162	Charles Pinckney (F)		14
1808	James Madison (DR)	Unknown	122	Charles Pinckney (F)		47
1812	James Madison (DR)	Unknown	128	De Witt Clinton (F)		89
1816	James Monroe (DR)	Unknown	183	Rufus King (F)		34
1820	James Monroe (DR)	Unknown	231	John Quincy Adams (DR)		1
1824	John Quincy Adams (NR)	105,321	84	Andrew Jackson (D)	155,872	99
				Henry Clay (DR)	46,587	37
				William H. Crawford (DR)	44,282	41
1828	Andrew Jackson (D)	647,276	178	John Quincy Adams (NR)	508,064	83
1832	Andrew Jackson (D)	687,502	219	Henry Clay (DR)	530,189	49
1836	Martin Van Buren (D)	762,678	170	William H. Harrison (W)	548,007	73
1840	William H. Harrison (W)	1,275,017	234	Martin Van Buren (D)	1,128,702	60
1844	James K. Polk (D)	1,337,243	170	Henry Clay (W)	1,299,068	105
1848	Zachary Taylor (W)	1,360,101	163	Lewis Cass (D)	1,220,544	127
1852	Franklin Pierce (D)	1,601,474	254	Winfield Scott (W)	1,386,578	42
1856	James C. Buchanan (D)	1,927,995	174	John C. Fremont (R)	1,391,555	114
1860	Abraham Lincoln (R)	1,866,352	180	Stephen A. Douglas (D)	1,375,157	12
				John C. Breckinridge (D)	845,763	72
1864	Abraham Lincoln (R)	2,216,067	212	George B. McClellan (D)	1,808,725	21
1868	Ulysses S. Grant (R)	3,015,071	214	Horatio Seymour (D)	2,709,615	80
1872	Ulysses S. Grant (R)	3,597,070	286	Horace Greeley (D)	2,834,079	

303

YEAR	PRESIDENTS ELECTED	POPULAR VOTE	ELECTORAL VOTE	DEFEATED CANDIDATES	POPULAR VOTE	ELECTORAL VOTE
1876	Rutherford B. Hayes (R)	4,033,950	185	Samuel J. Tilden (D)	4,284,855	184
1880	James A. Garfield (R)	4,449,053	214	Winfield S. Hancock (D)	4,442,030	155
1884	Grover Cleveland (D)	4,911,017	219	James G. Blaine (R)	4,848,334	182
1888	Benjamin Harrison (R)	5,440,216	233	Grover Cleveland (D)	5,538,233	168
1892	Grover Cleveland (D)	5,554,414	277	Benjamin Harrison (R)	5,190,802	145
				James Weaver (P)	1,027,329	22
1896	William McKinley (R)	7,035,638	271	William J. Bryan (D)	6,467,946	176
1900	William McKinley (R)	7,219,530	292	William J. Bryan (D)	6,358,071	155
1904	Theodore Roosevelt (R)	7,628,834	336	Alton B. Parker (D)	5,084,491	140
1908	William H. Taft (R)	7,679,006	321	William J. Bryan (D)	6,409,106	162
1912	Woodrow Wilson (D)	6,286,214	435	Theodore Roosevelt (Pr)	4,126,020	88
				William H. Taft (R)	3,483,922	8
1916	Woodrow Wilson (D)	9,129,606	277	Charles E. Hughes (R)	8,538,231	254
1920	Warren G. Harding (R)	16,152,200	404	James M. Cox (D)	9,147,553	127
1924	Calvin Coolidge (R)	15,725,016	382	John W. Davis (D)	8,386,503	136
				Robert M. LaFollette (Pr)	4,822,856	13
1928	Herbert Hoover (R)	21,429,109	444	Alfred E. Smith (D)	15,005,497	87
1932	Franklin D. Roosevelt (D)	22,851,857	472	Herbert Hoover (R)	15,761,841	59
1936	Franklin D. Roosevelt (D)	27,751,612	523	Alfred Landon (R)	16,679,583	8
1940	Franklin D. Roosevelt (D)	27,244,160	449	Wendell L. Willkie (R)	22,305,198	82
1944	Franklin D. Roosevelt (D)	25,602,504	432	Thomas E. Dewey (R)	22,014,201	99
1948	Harry S. Truman (D)	24,105,695	303	Thomas E. Dewey (R)	21,969,170	189
				J. Strom Thurmond (SR)	1,169,021	39
				Henry A. Wallace (Pr)	1,156,103	0
1952	Dwight D. Eisenhower (R)	33,936,252	442	Adlai E. Stevenson (D)	27,314,992	89

Presidents not listed above are John Tyler (1841–45), Millard Fillmore (1850–53), Andrew Johnson (1865–69), and Chester Arthur (1881–85), who attained the Presidency through the accident of death and were never elected to the office. T. Roosevelt, Coolidge and Truman, who also inherited the Presidency, were

Acknowledgments

The authors wish to express their particular gratitude to Miss Mary Cunningham of the New York State Historical Association for her valued assistance in the preparation of this book.

For their co-operation in supplying pictures and information we are greatly indebted to:

Clarence S. Brigham, American Antiquarian Society
Harry Collins, Brown Brothers
Alice Pickup, Buffalo Historical Society
Mrs. David Claire, Corcoran Gallery of Art
Florence Osborne and staff, Essex Institute
Herman Kahn and Grace Suckley, Franklin D. Roosevelt Library
Mrs. Henry W. Howell, Jr., and Helen Sanger, Frick Art Reference Library
Thomas Little, Harvard College Library
Rosanna Bagg and Mrs. Millicent Maybe, Huntington Memorial Library, Oneonta, New York
Carleton Thorpe, Peter A. Juley and Son
Virginia Daiker and Milton Kaplan, Library of Congress
Vera Andrus, Metropolitan Museum of Art
Mrs. Richard Kimball, American Museum of Natural History
Josephine Cobb, National Archives
Arthur Carlson, Caroline Scoon and Sylvester Vigilanti, New-York Historical Society
Louis C. Jones, New York State Historical Association
Wilson G. Duprez, William Mortenson, Saro J. Riccardi and Elizabeth E. Roth, New York Public Library
Sidney Solomon, Pageant Book Store
Margaret W. Brown and Mendel L. Petersen, Smithsonian Institution
Raymond B. Seymour, Sons of the Revolution
Mae Manning, Theodore Roosevelt Association
Edward August and Harold Feder, United Press Newspictures

Credits and References

CREDITS AND REFERENCES

CREDITS AND REFERENCES

67	bottom, left	New York Public Library.
67	bottom, right	Painting by François Auguste Baird, collection of Mr. George G. Frelinghuysen, courtesy Corcoran Gallery of Art.
68		Portrait by Henry Inman, source withheld by request of owner.
69	top	Essex Institute, Salem, Massachusetts.
69	bottom	The American Antiquarian Society, Worcester, Massachusetts.
70		Portrait by Henry Inman, courtesy The Art Commission of the City of New York.
71		*Ladies of the White House* by Laura C. Holloway.
72	top	Library of Congress.
72	center, right	*Connecticut Historical Collections,* New Haven, 1836.
72	bottom	Painting by James Henry Beard, courtesy Cincinnati Art Museum.
73	both	Library of Congress.
74		Portrait by Abel Nichols, courtesy Essex Institute.
75		*Perley's Reminiscences* by Benjamin Perley Poore, Vol. I.
76		New-York Historical Society.
77	top	Library of Congress.
77	bottom	Essex Institute.
78		Silhouette by William H. Brown.
79	left	*Ladies of the White House* by Laura C. Holloway.
79	right	Portrait by Francesco Anelli, White House Collection, courtesy Frick Art Reference Library.
80 & 81	top	Library of Congress.
80	top, left	Library of Congress.
80	bottom	Bettmann Archive.
81	top, right	New York Public Library.
81	center, left	New York Public Library.
81	bottom, right	Artist unknown, courtesy Indiana University Library.
82		Portrait by Thomas Sully, courtesy American Scenic and Historic Preservation Society.
83		*Ladies of the White House* by Laura C. Holloway.
84		*Illustrated London News,* 1845.
85	left	*Yankee Doodle,* 1846.
85	right	New York Public Library.
86	top, left	Library of Congress.
86	top, right	New York Public Library.
86	center, right	Library of Congress.
86	bottom, left	Copyright Winthrop-Stearns Inc.
87	top, left	Library of Congress.
87	top, right	Library of Congress.
87	bottom, left	Author's collection.
87	bottom, right	Library of Congress.
88		Library of Congress.
89	top	Metropolitan Museum of Art.
89	bottom	Library of Congress.
90	top	New-York Historical Society.
90	bottom	Library of Congress.
91	top	Metropolitan Museum of Art.
91	bottom	Library of Congress.

PAGE	POSITION	
92	top	Painting by Henry Boese, courtesy Museum of the City of New York.
92	right	Artist unknown, courtesy Wells Fargo Bank and Trust Company, San Francisco.
92	bottom	*Illustrated London News,* June 2, 1849.
93	top	New-York Historical Society.
93	left	Library of Congress.
93	bottom, right	Painting by Linton Park, collection of Mr. and Mrs. Edgar Garbisch, courtesy National Gallery of Art.
94		Buffalo Historical Society.
95	top two	*Life of Millard Fillmore,* published by R. M. DeWitt, courtesy Buffalo Historical Society.
95	bottom	Buffalo Historical Society.
96	top, left	Smithsonian Institution.
96	top, right	*Gleason's Pictorial,* May 10, 1851.
96	bottom	*Gleason's Pictorial,* July 7, 1851.
97	all three	Buffalo Historical Society.
98	top, left	New-York Historical Society.
98	right	*Harper's New Monthly Magazine,* August, 1851.
98	bottom, left	Detail of painting by James E. Butterworth, courtesy Museum of Art, Rhode Island School of Design.
99	all three	Library of Congress.
100		*Illustrated News,* 1853.
101		Portrait by G. P. A. Healy, courtesy New-York Historical Society.
102	top	*Gleason's Pictorial,* March 11, 1854.
102	bottom	*Ladies of the White House* by Laura C. Holloway.
103		*Gleason's Pictorial,* June 11, 1853.
104	top, left	Library of Congress.
104	center, right	Library of Congress.
104	bottom, left	New Bedford Public Library.
104	bottom, right	*Gleason's Pictorial,* 1855.
105	top, both	Library of Congress.
105	bottom, left	*The Lantern,* 1852.
105	bottom, right	Painting by H. M. T. Powell, collection of Mr. and Mrs. Edwin Grabhorn, courtesy Corcoran Gallery of Art.
106		*Vanity Fair.*
107		Portrait by W. E. McMaster, courtesy American Scenic and Historic Preservation Society.
108		*Harper's New Monthly Magazine,* April, 1857.
109	top	Library of Congress.
109	bottom	*A History of the United States,* by Benjamin Lossing.
110	all three	Library of Congress.
111	top, left	Library of Congress.
111	top, right	*Harper's Weekly,* May 5, 1860.
111	bottom	Painting by Thomas Pritchard Rossiter, courtesy Smithsonian Institution, National Collection of Fine Arts.
112		Portrait by Lafond, source withheld by request of owner, courtesy Frick Art Reference Library.
113	top	*Vanity Fair,* April 7, 1860.
113	bottom	*Echoes of the Rocky Mountains,* 1868, by J. W. Clampitt.
114		*Punch,* June 7, 1862.
115		Library of Congress.

CREDITS AND REFERENCES

CREDITS AND REFERENCES

CREDITS AND REFERENCES

PAGE	POSITION	
249	top, right	Museum of Modern Art.
249	bottom, left	Rollin Kirby, New York *World,* from New York Public Library.
249	bottom, right	United Press.
250		Brown Brothers.
251		United Press.
252	top	Portrait by Edmund Tarbelle, courtesy Smithsonian Institution.
252	bottom	United Press.
253		Library of Congress.
254	top	United Press.
254	bottom	Rollin Kirby, New York *World,* from New York Public Library.
255		United Press.
256	all three	United Press.
257	left	United Press.
257	top, right	National Archives.
257	bottom, right	United Press.
258		Franklin D. Roosevelt Library, Hyde Park, New York
259		Franklin D. Roosevelt Library.
260		Franklin D. Roosevelt Library.
261	both	Franklin D. Roosevelt Library.
262	both	Franklin D. Roosevelt Library.
263		Franklin D. Roosevelt Library.
264	top	Franklin D. Roosevelt Library.
264	bottom	Lute Pease, courtesy New York Public Library.
265	top, left	Acme, from Franklin D. Roosevelt Library.
265	top center, top right, and bottom two	Franklin D. Roosevelt Library.
266		Franklin D. Roosevelt Library.
267		Signal Corps, from Franklin D. Roosevelt Library.
268	all three	United Press.
269	all four	United Press.
270	top	Signal Corps, from Franklin D. Roosevelt Library.
270	bottom	D. R. Fitzpatrick, courtesy St. Louis *Post-Dispatch.*
271		Franklin D. Roosevelt Library.
272		United Press.
273	left	Copyright, Hessler, from United Press.
273	right	United Press.
274	top	United Press.
274	bottom	Photo by Frank Cancellare, from United Press.
275	all three	United Press.
276	top	D. R. Fitzpatrick, courtesy St. Louis *Post-Dispatch.*
276	bottom	United Press.
277		United Press.
278	top	National Archives.
278	bottom, left	United Press.
278	right	National Archives.
279	top and bottom, left	United Press.
279	bottom, right	United States Lines, New York.
280	top	Photo by Abbie Rowe, courtesy National Park Service.

CREDITS AND REFERENCES

PAGE	POSITION	
280	bottom	Metropolitan Museum of Art.
281	all three	Photo by Abbie Rowe, courtesy National Park Service.
282		United Press.
283		United Press.
284		European Picture Service.
285		United Press.
286		United Press.
287		United Press.
288		United Press.
289		Painting by Thomas Stevens, courtesy National Park Service.
290	all three	United Press.
291	bottom, left	United Press.
291	bottom, right	*The Washington Star.*
292	all three	United Press.
293	top	United Press.
293	bottom	*The Newark Evening News.*

Index

323